PAT TAYLOR WAS ONLY 38 YEARS OLD. SHE WASN'T READY TO DIE.

When she came to the Arizona Heart Institute, she was taking 38 prescribed pills a day, could barely draw her breath, and was suffering from extreme angina pain. She had survived two heart attacks, three catheterizations, two open-heart surgeries, two bypass grafts, enormous dosages of medicine, and confusing diagnoses. The last medical advice she received was to "go home to Long Island and die."

But Pat Taylor was only 38 years old. She wasn't ready to die. With the support of her husband and two sons, Pat went to the Arizona Heart Institute, where the Diethrich program was created for her—a strict regimen of diet, exercise, and counseling which restored Pat's health and returned her to a pain-free, drug-free life.

For every inspiring story like Pat Taylor's, there are millions of Americans who are in the dark, who are unaware of the risks of heart disease, and—more importantly—the ways to reduce them. This book is for you. The explanations and guidelines that follow tell you what *you can do* to help improve the quality of your life.

Take *The Heart Test* now—before it's too late.

It's a program that can make a difference in your life.

Ask Pat Taylor.

The Heart Test

Dr. Edward B. Diethrich

BANTAM BOOKS
TORONTO • NEW YORK • LONDON • SYDNEY • AUCKLAND

Our sincere appreciation to Bantam Books for the use of their film in the production of these books.

*This low-priced Bantam Book
has been completely reset in a type face
designed for easy reading, and was printed
from new plates. It contains the complete
text of the original hard-cover edition.*
NOT ONE WORD HAS BEEN OMITTED.

THE ARIZONA HEART INSTITUTE'S HEART TEST

*A Bantam Book / published by arrangement with
Cornerstone Library*

PRINTING HISTORY
Cornerstone Library edition published November 1981
Bantam edition / May 1983

ISBN 0-553-23202-9

Published simultaneously in the United States and Canada

Bantam Books are published by Bantam Books, Inc. Its trademark, consisting of the words "Bantam Books" and the portrayal of a rooster, is Registered in U.S. Patent and Trademark Office and in other countries. Marca Registrada. Bantam Books, Inc., 666 Fifth Avenue, New York, New York 10103.

PRINTED IN THE UNITED STATES OF AMERICA

O   0 9 8 7 6 5 4 3 2 1

Contents

Preface
Acknowledgments

Part I: Discovering Your Risks

1. The Pat Taylor Story   5
2. Knowing Your Heart   19
3. Who Are You?   25
4. The Heart Test   35
5. Now What?   43

Part II: Reducing Your Risks

6. The Smoking Factor   53
7. The Stress Factor   75
8. The Weight Factor   111
9. The Diet Factor   151
10. The Exercise Factor   187

Part III: Conclusion

11. From Around the Nation   223

Index   229

Preface

Heart disease afflicts over forty million people in this country. This year alone, one million of those people will die, more than half from heart attack. Many will be struck down without even a warning sign. Furthermore, other industrialized countries are experiencing an increase in heart disease as their life-styles become more complex and "Westernized."

Ten years ago, a group of deeply concerned, industrious, farsighted medical professionals, businessmen, and benefactors were drawn together by their common interest in fighting this worldwide disease. The result of this meeting was the inception of the International Heart Foundation, a nonprofit organization chartered to sponsor research and education in the field of cardiovascular medicine. At this same time, another organization was born—the Arizona Heart Institute, a medical center for the diagnosis and treatment of heart disease. Together, the IHF and the AHI have been working over the decade to conquer a common foe.

At first, progress was slow. The Arizona Heart Institute, then housed in a Phoenix hospital, began to build a reputation for outstanding patient care and pioneering diagnostic and therapeutic modalities. Over the years, the Institute's reputation grew and with it the need to expand. Soon an independent building was constructed to house the facility. Designed under the auspices of the International Heart Foundation to ensure that only the most advanced instrumentation and health care delivery concepts were employed, this structure became the nation's first freestanding outpatient diagnostic and treatment center for heart disease. Now, some three years later, the Institute is deeply committed to clinical research and has amassed a data base of medical information upon which its researchers can draw.

The Foundation and the Institute both are dedicated to improving medical care through research and education. As such, they strive to revolutionize and innovate rather than copy. As the medical information stored at the Institute grew, it became clear that there were trends among patients which could be identified and categorized. These trends became known as risk factors, and other investigators in the field as well were studying the applicability of these trends to the prediction of heart disease. The Foundation conceived the idea of taking these risk factors and compiling a form that would allow the Institute's physicians to report to a patient his risk of developing heart disease based on the results of the patient's diagnostic tests. In turn, this analysis form could then be used as an input sheet for computerization of the findings and statistical analyses of the trends. For two years or more, this risk factor analysis form has been used in the Institute, continually being modified to make it a more accurate, useful clinical tool and an easily understood, informative guideline for the patient.

Because the Foundation is as much dedicated to education as to its research goals, the board of trustees wished to condense the risk factor analysis into a short list of questions whose answers could be scored and the total score related to the participant's risk of heart disease—low, medium, or high. This questionnaire then became the basis of the nationally televised "Great American Heart Test." This segment of ABC News' "20/20" program was unprecedented for two reasons. It marked the first time that television had been used to conduct a health survey, and it drew the largest audience response to any show in ABC News history—over 250,000 pieces of mail, mostly answers to the test, were received and delivered to the Foundation. Although caught somewhat off guard by the deluge of responses, the Foundation sprang into action, mounting a tremendous volunteer effort to read, answer, and computerize the answers. At the present time, a team of medical experts and biostatisticians are poring over the results in preparation for their final report, expected late this fall.

However, the Foundation's board learned much more from the Heart Test than just the scores of a quarter million people. They realized that the American public is thirsty for information, eager to learn about their health and do something about it. In this day of joggers and health enthusiasts, it seems most appropriate that the Heart Test should offer to these people a means of identifying the health status of their hearts. And so this book was born out of the Foundation's desire to fill the needs of the public, and to educate people to achieve healthier, longer lives.

This book was designed for you *to use*. Merely skimming the pages will not do. You must actively take part and become involved in your health. By answering the self-test questions, you will gain an appreciation of what you are doing to your body—both the good and the bad. The explanations and guidelines that follow will tell you what you may do to help improve the quality of your life.

Acknowledgments

Obviously a book such as this, covering diverse fields of knowledge, is truly a product of the Arizona Heart Institute, not any one person. I am deeply indebted to the many people who have contributed their time, interest, and expertise to making The Heart Test and our heart-care program into an attractive and usable book for the average reader. My thanks go to Dewey D. Schade, Gregory J. Petras, Jayne Lapidus, Sheila Coonen, David Hall, Steve Harrison, Dick Williams, Natalie Winthrop, John DeForest, Dan Timmons, Jill Johnson, Bess Maxwell, Jane Thropp, Paula Banahan, Julie Adams, Penny Laner, and Diane Diehl.

Special thanks go to Tom Cowan of New York for coordinating the project, researching our program and developing the text. Without his contribution this book could not have been created.

PART I

Discovering Your Risks

The Heart Test in this book may change your life. It may also save your life.

When it first appeared on ABC's "20/20" program in February 1981, an incredible thing happened. An estimated twenty-five million Americans watched the program, and of that number, a quarter of a million people, over 260,000, sent in their results. As moderator Hugh Downs indicated, we will never know just how many viewers actually took the self-assessment test and discovered their chances of developing heart disease. Probably never before in the history of medicine have so many Americans been aware of their own personal risk factors that could lead to heart attacks and strokes.

The quarter of a million viewers who sent in their results did so to help further our research into the causes and prevention of cardiovascular disease. Many asked about their hearts and requested advice and more information from us at the Arizona Heart Institute. They sent in their scores and questions on the backs of old envelopes, scraps of paper, pieces of cardboard, paper plates, whatever they happened to have handy by the TV. One family—eating a box of valentine candy—took the test on the lid, realized their own risks, threw out the rest of the candy, and sent us their score on the empty box! These viewers were promised no prizes, no coupons, no gimmicks, nor, on this program, were they promised a preventive program for reducing their heart risks and thereby extending their chances for a long and healthy life.

The book you now hold is that preventive program.

Created by the Arizona Heart Institute over the last ten years, this program has helped over a hundred thousand people from all walks of life and every section of the country to enjoy a fuller, more active life. Many were at high risk levels when they came to us. Many had had previous heart attacks and heart surgery. Some came simply to prevent heart problems in the future. We know from experience that our program works. It worked for them, and it can work for you.

Using the most advanced and sophisticated testing procedures that are technologically available, we can predict with a high degree of reliability who the future heart victims are most likely to be. But *you* don't need to go to a heart clinic at this point to assess your chances of having a heart attack. The Heart Test in this book is your first step to finding out whether or not you may end up a heart victim yourself. By taking this Heart Test, you can derive a realistic assessment of your own chances of suffering from cardiovascular problems. The test will indicate whether your chances for heart disease are dangerously high, or medium, or that they are low and you are relatively safe.

1 The Pat Taylor Story

When Pat Taylor came to the Arizona Heart Institute in Phoenix, she was no novice to heart disease. She had seen cardiologists and surgeons in New York and Texas, had been in and out of waiting rooms, emergency rooms, cardiac care units, and rehabilitation programs. She *knew* her heart, having lived more intimately with it in pain and suffering for the previous seventeen months than most of us will in a lifetime. Her excruciating battle with angina, beginning just before Christmas in 1978, finally led to two heart attacks, three catheterizations, two open-heart surgeries, two bypass grafts, enormous dosages of medications, and disappointing diet and exercise therapies—all with the same result: Nothing worked. Pat had seen a lot, tried a lot, suffered a lot.

When she finally arrived in Arizona in May 1980, she was taking thirty-eight pills a day, some in dangerously high dosages. She could not climb the stairs in the lobby of the Heart Institute. She could barely draw her breath. She was still in pain. Months of unceasing cardiac treatment had not returned Pat to anything resembling her normal life. That she was still alive, she was grateful. The last medical advice she received from a well-known heart clinic was, in her words, "Nothing can be done. Go home to Long Island and die." Pat Taylor was thirty-eight years old. She wasn't ready to die.

Her husband, Richie, and their two sons did not want her to die, either. Together they had persevered so long and valiantly through the long months of pain and worry that began that Thursday night in December when Pat came home from a meeting, lay down on the bed, a bit tired, and felt her first siege of angina rip across her chest and down her arms. It went through her with such unbelievable fury that for an hour and a half she wanted someone to tear her arms from her body to give her relief. Her husband gave her some aspirin to ease the pain. When it finally subsided, she fell asleep. But on Friday another siege hit her and the following day she was hospitalized.

Pat Taylor didn't know it at the time, but later she would find that one of her major coronary arteries had a 98 percent blockage. Pat's condition was a perfect example of accelerated atheroslcerosis, an advanced condition normally not found in so young a person.

Thus began Pat's long and unrelenting ordeal with doctors, tests, drugs, confusing diagnoses, prescriptions, and expensive health care treatments. It all came as a sudden shock, since she had never suspected that she was a potential heart victim. She had always thought of herself as healthy, not having needed to see a doctor in the four years prior to the pains in her chest. Even when her husband rushed her back to a New York hospital the day after her first visit, the doctor who had done the electrocardiogram on her was surprised to see her again. "The little girl who thinks she has heart trouble," he called her. As with so many heart victims, no one knew.

If Pat had taken the Heart Test, her score would have been 57, that is, extremely high. The telltale risk factors were there. Pat's mother had died of a heart attack at the age of thirty-nine. Pat's uncle also died of heart attack and her brother had diabetes. Pat had smoked two and a half packs of cigarettes a day for about ten years, although she had quit cold turkey when a close friend died of cancer. She admits she has Type A or AA behavior. She never closely watched her diet. As she said, "No one knew. Not even myself."

In her strange odyssey back to health, Pat was told misleading and sometimes conflicting things by the doctors who were treating her. She was told by one doctor that she had nothing but a pinched muscle. Another suggested her problem was heartburn. At one point she was given a prescription for such a high dosage of medicine that a Long Island pharmacist refused to fill it. Later a second doctor advised that aspirin was all she needed. She was told that one of her coronary arteries was 50 percent blocked but that she should accept it as 50 percent open and live with it that way. A later opinion was that the half-blocked artery would require a bypass operation.

ABC NEWS—ARIZONA HEART INSTITUTE CARDIOVASCULAR RISK FACTOR ANALYSIS

		Score	
1. Age	Age 56 or over	1	
	Age 55 or younger	0	0
2. Sex	Male	1	
	Female	0	0
3. Family History	If you have: Blood relatives who have had a heart attack or stroke *before* age 60	12	
	Blood relatives with a known history of heart disease at or before age 60 but no heart attacks or stroke	10	
	Blood relatives who have had a heart attack or stroke *after* age 60	6	
	No blood relatives who have had a heart attack or stroke	0	12
4. Personal History	*50 and under:* If you have had either a heart attack, a stroke, heart or blood vessel surgery ...	20	
	51 and over: If you have had any of the above	10	
	None of the above	0	20

Score

5. Diabetes

Diabetes *before age 40* and now on insulin **10**

Diabetes *at or after age 40* and now on insulin or pills **5**

If your diabetes is controlled by diet, or your diabetes began *after age 55* **3**

If you have never had diabetes . **0** **0**

6. Smoking

Two packs per day **10**

Between one and two packs per day *or* quit smoking *less than a year ago* **6**

If you smoke 6 or more cigars a day or inhale a pipe regularly .. **6**

Less than one pack per day *or* quit smoking more than a year ago . **3**

Never smoked **0** **3**

7. Cholesterol
(If cholesterol count is not known answer 8)

Cholesterol level—276 or above **10**

Cholesterol level—between 225 and 275 .... **5**

Cholesterol level—224 or below . **0** **10**

8. Diet
(If you've answered 7, do not answer 8)

Does your normal eating pattern include:

One serving of red meat daily, more than seven eggs a week, and daily consumption of butter, whole milk, and cheese ... **8**

Red meat 4–6 times a week, 4–7 eggs a week, margarine, low fat dairy products, and some cheese **4**

Poultry, fish, little or no red meat, three or fewer eggs a week, some margarine, skim milk, and skim milk products .... **0** ___

<u>Score</u>

9. High Blood Pressure	If *either* number is: 160 over 100 (160/100) or higher 140 over 90 (140/90) but less than 160 over 100 (160/100) .... If *both* numbers are *less than* 140 over 90 (140/90)	10 5 0 <u>0</u>

10. Weight	Ideal Weight Formula:
	    Men = 110 lbs. plus 5 lbs. for
	each inch over 5 feet
	    Women = 100 lbs. plus 5 lbs.
	for each inch over 5 feet
	25 pounds overweight ....
	10 to 24 pounds overweight ....
	Less than 10 pounds overweight
		
		4
		2
		0 <u>4</u>

11. Exercise	Do you engage in any aerobic ex- ercise (brisk walking, jogging, bicycling, racketball, swimming) for *more than 15 minutes:* Less than once a week .... 1 to 2 times a week .... 3 or more times a week	 4 2 0 <u>4</u>

12. Stress	Are you:
	    Frustrated when waiting in line,
	    often in a hurry to complete
	    work or keep appointments,
	    easily angered, irritable .....
	    Impatient when waiting, *occa-
	    ionally* hurried, or *occasionally*
	    moody ....
	    Comfortable when waiting,
	    seldom rushed, and easygoing
		
		4
		
		2
		
		0 <u>4</u>

TOTAL POINTS: <u>57</u>

Pat had her first actual heart attack in a recovery room in Texas after her second open-heart surgery. She had a second heart attack when she returned to N.Y., which the doctor refused to tell her about. She says she actually died in that recovery room and they "pulled me back with the paddles." In New York she was referred back to a Texas clinic for what would be her third bypass operation because they suspected her graft was once again closing. But when she went back to Texas, the report given her was that her arteries were too small and that she was not a candidate for another operation. They would ''lose you on the table'' is the way they put it to her.

When she was told that she would have to learn to ''live with a little pain,'' she grew defiant and told her doctor he was wrong. ''I'm having pain that isn't right,'' she told him. ''I'm not supposed to live with this!'' Her only hope was to go to California for a heart transplant. ''No way!'' she responded. ''I don't want my heart taken out and someone else's put in.'' She was thinking of the rather dismal success rate since the ''transplant era'' began back in the late sixties. She also had to consider the intense pain and emotional trauma she and her family would have to go through. Discouraged and frightened, Pat returned home once again with her prescriptions for Inderal, which her New York doctor decided to *reduce* so that if she continued to suffer angina, he would be able to *increase* the dosage. To Pat it seemed she was on a medical roller coaster of cures and treatments, a roller coaster doomed to jump the track.

So the months passed. Pat was determined to live. ''I've got to raise these boys,'' she decided. ''My mother died and left a whole bunch of kids.'' But the pain began again in the winter, and she once again ended up in the emergency room, this time on Saint Patrick's Day in 1980. It was at this time, when she was told that a transplant was her last hope, that she considered contacting us at the Arizona Heart Institute because of an article she had read on what we were doing, the different approaches we were taking, and what seemed to her at the time a better ''last hope.'' As it turned out, it was.

Pat came to us weighing 153 pounds, far too heavy for her petite five-foot-four-inch frame. Her cholesterol level was 351. You will learn from the Heart Test in chapter 4 where that put her in terms of risk. She was gulping down medication like it was lemonade in the hot desert sun. Her breathing was erratic. She could barely walk without pain. We immediately introduced her to a battery of noninvasive screening procedures that we have administered on an outpatient basis to hundreds of people from across the country. With these results in hand, I broke the news to Pat and her husband.

''I could operate on you,'' I told her, ''but the results would be dismal. But I think we can help you without another operation." I then asked her if she would stay with us for eight weeks.

I still remember the look on her face when she heard this, a look of disbelief and distrust created by months of conflicting diagnoses and cures that crisscrossed from Long Island to Houston. And now Phoenix. "No," she answered. "If I'm going to die, I don't want to be away from my husband and sons." I don't remember how I told her that I didn't think she had to die, but today Pat claims I said something about a bus running over her when she's eighty. Perhaps I did. The important thing was that Richie said she was staying, and so Pat stayed, and the staff at the Arizona Heart Institute created for her what we now call the Diethrich Program, an extremely strict regiment of diet, exercise, and counseling that restored Pat's health and returned her to a painfree, drugfree life.

We knew from years of experience that the most complete program for rehabilitating heart patients must be a multidisciplinary one. Surgical techniques and the appropriate medical management alone will not do it. Neither will exercises or diets without a systematic philosophy behind them that includes behavior modification, so that a person restructures his or her life-style, and does not merely add a few exercises here and a few restricted meals there. Even though modern science has made great strides in preventing, detecting, and treating cardiovascular diseases, it is not always science alone that brings about the most satisfactory cures—if we can even call them cures. A heart victim, like Pat and others, will tell you years after they have resumed normal living that they are still victims. Bypass surgery, for example, does just that—it bypasses the problem. It is not a cure. A cure for atherosclerosis has not yet been found. Pat, like so many others, is still a heart victim, much like a reformed alcoholic who will continue to describe himself or herself as an alcoholic. Heart disease might, and does, recur.

It may seem a bit unorthodox that a heart surgeon should devise and promote a nonsurgical program to combat the effects of atherosclerosis. But this very recurrence of angina and heart attacks in postoperative patients calls for methods that go beyond what relief can be accomplished in the operating room. It is clear to me that until medical science discovers a genuine cure for atherosclerosis, we must provide our patients with the most complete nonsurgical methods to prevent future attacks after their operations. In the case of high-risk candidates, we must make available the same methods to prevent their ever needing surgery. We can remove atherosclerotic plaque from an endangered artery, we can graft an additional vein around it, but once the patient leaves the hospital, the removal of disease-generating habits and the grafting of healthy ones must continue in his or her individual life. Without such a program, our work as heart surgeons will end in frustration.

The Diethrich Program was devised for people with severe forms of atherosclerosis, people whose condition cannot be easily improved or controlled by the gamut of sophisticated technology and medications, diets, and exercise programs that are currently available. Sometimes it is not until we have patients opened on the table in the operating room that we learn how extensive their disease is. What we thought was blockage of one artery turns out to include several, and often arteries on which we cannot operate because, like Pat's, they are too small or too filled with atherosclerotic debris. On the long continuum of coronary heart disease, surgery is just one component. For people like them a postoperative program is a necessity if they hope to return to active lives. There are also people with markedly abnormal biochemical factors for which surgery offers nothing. Obviously in their cases the heart surgeon must have other remedies to offer. Similarly, young people, like Pat, with accelerated atherosclerosis must be given hope that the years ahead will not see a recurrence of bypass surgery and the trauma it inflicts both physically and mentally. Lastly, we believe the Diethrich Program is for those people who have tried the other approaches offered elsewhere and have found them wanting, as well as for people just discovering that they are at high risk for coronary disease and that for the rest of their lives they will have to live with the strictest precaution for their hearts.

The Diethrich Program, even though it is shaped individually as we apply it to each patient, must be adaptable to the patient's family also. It consists of a total life-style that includes to a lesser extent all the members of the family. Heart victims need the support of their loved ones; they need to think that their strictly controlled way of life is compatible with family customs and rituals. The constraints of economy alone would suggest that for the family to be on one diet would make more sense and utilize the food budget more efficiently than to provide for several diets. In short, as Pat's husband and sons were soon to learn, Pat's heart was their heart too.

The multidisciplinary program that we offer consists of five phases: nutrition management, exercise, stress reduction and behavioral change, medical monitoring, and practical instructions on how to stay on the program after a patient leaves the Heart Institute. The members of our staff who participate in the Diethrich Program and work most closely with our patients include cardiologists, nutritionists, psychologists, exercise physiologists, and registered nurses. Many of our staff hold multiple degrees and come to the Arizona Heart Institute with a wide background of experiences in cardiovascular treatment. Together we have created a cardiac rehabilitation program that penetrates into every area of the patient's life-style. Together, and with the cooperation of the heart patients themselves, we can introduce heart victims to a positive way of life that frequently matches the joy and enthusiasm of their former lives in many ways.

The specific goal of our program is to reduce the clinical symptoms of heart disease by systematically modifying and reducing the risk factors that lead to life-threatening disabilities, the same risk factors that you will rate yourself on when taking the Heart Test. How do we it?

First, we must identify those risk factors. We proceed by performing more extensive testing and screening in our labs. We include resting ECGs and stress ECGs on a treadmill. We run complete blood analyses to determine the patient's blood values (cholesterol and triglyceride levels, HDLs, etc.). If needed, we then bring out the "heavy equipment," the nuclear scanning and the catheterization instrumentation. With the results from all these tests, we can compile the most complete profile of the patient's heart condition. When this is done, we decide whether a patient falls within the select group that could benefit from the Diethrich Program. If so, we then develop a personalized prescription for the individual.

We first provide participants with a new outlook on food. What you eat is so important to your overall health that to ignore a carefully selected diet, prepared to supplement the body's own life-restoring powers, would counteract the benefits of any other remedy. A personalized diet is a must. So through extensive education about nutrition, our patients learn the components of a low-fat, low-sodium, low-refined-carbohydrate diet. What's more, they learn how to prepare for themselves and their families meals that are not dull and tasteless.

When I called in our nutritionist for consultation about Pat Taylor's program, we agreed from the very start that the Diethrich Diet would have to be varied and interesting enough that Pat and her family would want to come to meals and enjoy them and, most of all, that it would be a diet that the family would *stay* on. So many programs, like the Pritikin one, are fine if the patient is confined to a high-pressure environment where there is considerable peer pressure and artificial motivation to follow the diet. But what happens when they leave? Our experience is that many go right back to their old eating habits, disregarding the risk factors that once again increase their chances for another, possibly fatal, attack.

As our patients learn the Diethrich Diet, they set for themselves the two-part goals of achieving and then maintaining their ideal weight. By measuring skin folds at six different sites on your body, we can determine what percentage of your mass is body fat. There are desirable and undesirable ranges. Even without the graduated skin clamp that measures your fat folds, you can make a pretty good estimate of your own by looking in the mirror—sideways.

Another essential goal achieved through our diet program is lowering and controlling elevated blood pressure. Diet, weight reduction, and sometimes medication are necessary, as Pat discovered in her own case. To leave out diet or exercise or initial medication destroys the effectiveness of what must be a multifaceted program. Eventually, through careful medical monitoring, medication dosages are reduced and eliminated. Today one year after she began our program, Pat is on absolutely no medication. Her blood pressure is normal. She feels no pain.

Pat's recovery was remarkable but not unbelievable. We believe in the cooperative effort of patients and health care professionals to bring the patient back to a higher quality of life. At the Arizona Heart Institute we see the results of this belief every day. There is nothing mysterious about it. Sound information about diet, exercise, typical everyday stress and how these affect your cardiovascular condition is the essential road map to a painfree life. Our patients learn techniques to manage stress and reduce it as a risk factor. They learn to establish long- and short-term life goals consistent with their values, abilities, interests, and heart conditions. They learn how to quit smoking, how to relax, how to manage their time. In short, they learn how to live in such a way that they unlock their inner strengths for dealing with the world as it is and the demands that world makes upon them and their hearts. They learn it is possible to take that alarmingly high Heart Test score and with diligence and perseverance drive it down to the middle- and eventually low-risk range.

When Pat Taylor left our program at the end of May 1980, after eight weeks, she had lost sixteen pounds. She was performing ten different calisthenics, each for a half minute. She was riding a stationary bike for ten minutes at a mild but significant resistance, considering the fact that she could not pedal without chest pains and shortness of breath eight weeks earlier. She was lifting three-pound weights for three minutes. She could complete the stair-climbing exercise comfortably and walk at a brisk pace up an incline. Pat's peak heart rate while she exercised reached 158 beats per minute, compared with the 84 she could achieve only with the greatest difficulty two months before.

What thrilled Pat most of all, more than the measurements and statistical profiles, was the simple, human joy of exercising without pain. "It seemed unreal," she now recalls. "I actually enjoyed my routines, whereas the rehab program I was on in New York caused me to regress! Back there, not only was I growing less able to pedal the bike at my original tension, I was in pain. The Arizona program helped me progress, and it killed my pain, instead of the pain killing me."

Today Pat is living proof that both the art and the science of medicine can work if the right people, with the right attitude, determine to make them work. Pat's objective evaluation, what we might call the "science of medicine," measured under our clinical auspices, is excellent. Although her resting ECG indicates the damage from her previous two heart attacks, her present ECG on the treadmill shows no abnormalities under physical stress, no arrhythmias, and a normal blood pressure response to the exercise. Her endurance and intensity show a high performance level. Today Pat can exercise into stage four of the Bruce Protocol, one of the most difficult treadmill tests, and one not usually given for heart rehabilitation. Nuclear scans indicate she is receiving more blood to her heart, not less. The cholesterol, triglyceride, HDL, and sugar levels in her blood have all responded dramatically. She now weighs 118, the ideal weight we prescribed for her from skinfold tests. Not only has she achieved this weight, but she has maintained it over the year. The much-hoped-for result that all of these data point to was confirmed by Pat's recent catheterization: there has been no progression of atherosclerosis over the past year. As one of our exercise physi-ologists put it, "It's phenomenal for a woman with her past medical history to be able to exercise at high levels without bringing on the symptoms that she did at lower levels a year previously." But in simple terms, Pat has eliminated those symp-toms by eliminating or reducing the risk factors that brought those symptoms on. And what is Pat's Heart Test score today? Thirty-five total points, in the medium range, contrasted with the high-risk level of 57 just a year ago.

Furthermore, a subjective evaluation of Pat's condition, what we can attribute to the "art of medicine," the proof she discov-ers in her daily life at home, is also excellent. She is free of pain. She is no longer on medication. She jogs two miles in twenty minutes, more easily, she claims, than her husband. She plays racketball, rides a stationary bike in her home at thirty-five to forty miles an hour for twenty minutes. She holds a full-time job selling insurance, has no maid or cook, does all the house-work, belongs to several civic organizations in which she holds offices and which take up three or four evenings a week in meetings. You can see that she is still a Type A person, but she has learned to make it work for her, instead of against her, with proper stress-reduction techniques and relaxation methods.

Her only discomfort occurs occasionally when she tries to lift heavy things, and this is pain in her chest where she had surgical stitches, not in her heart. Sometimes on cold, windy nights on Long Island, the winter air brings with it a little angina. But it is not severe. If she is around someone who is smoking, she is conscious of her oxygen supply being reduced. And occasionally she experiences a "skippy," a momentary loss of air, which she has come to appreciate as an old friend who warns her that even though she has made a remarkable recovery, she is still a heart victim. "The skippies are not frightening. It isn't painful. It's like a silent hiccup. The breath just isn't there. And I think it's healthy to be reminded of what I owe my heart," she explains.

She knows what will happen should she ever forget. "Every so often I used to think, 'Oh, I'm well,' and I'd go off my exercises and get into trouble. I went off for three weeks once and didn't do any exercises and I started having pains again and not feeling well. Boy, did I get scared, really scared. I'll never do it again.'' She admits that once in a while she cheats on her diet, usually a craving for something sweet. But Pat knows that it's okay, as she says, ''once in a blue moon'' to have a fling. The important thing is that she is not in the *habit* of cheating. She and her family stay on the diet. She boasts that her family of four eats only one pound of meat a day and has a weekly grocery bill that hovers around seventy dollars. ''And we eat *well*. We've eliminated the garbage stuff, the junk food.'' Even her sons have learned to regulate their diets along Pat's program. How does she explain it to her friends? ''When it's a matter of life or death, it's pretty motivating. For all of us. After all, the boys may have inherited a tendency toward heart disease from me.''

It is extremely important that Pat's subjective feelings match the objective printouts from her screening tests here at the Heart Institute. What she does at home, how she lives in New York, the way she can respond to her family and friends, are all important for health. A healthy mind in a healthy body is still the best description of holistic health. What good would it be if her ECG and nuclear scans and triglyceride levels all read ''healthy'' and yet her enthusiasm and zest for a life with vitality, factors that can't really be measured, were pitifully low? At the Arizona Heart Institute we believe it is important to bring the quality of life into optimal levels. We believe it is absolutely necessary that an ''excellent'' recovery report include your ability to go back to work and play, to enjoy hobbies, sports, and sex, to pursue the family life you once knew. Stress, anxiety, or worry over any of these, even one's hobby or sex life, can trigger angina. In short, what is really at stake is our total self, our total life. To paraphrase John F. Kennedy, eternal vigilance is the price we must pay for a healthy life.

Pat Taylor pays that price. She does her family. If the price seems high to you, who have not had to redeem so much of your own life from the clutches of atherosclerosis, it does not seem that high a price to Pat. As she told us here recently when she returned for her first year's checkup, ''It upsets me deeply that people in this country do not take heart disease as the number one killer. Everyone goes around thinking their hearts are fine, and they do all the wrong things, eat the wrong things, live the wrong way. And people who do have heart disease think they should just lie down and die. Especially men. They feel it's just too much effort to want to live. I get very upset when I hear that.''

Pat has learned, as we all do sooner or later, but perhaps in less dramatic ways, that the important parts of life are often those we take for granted, never realizing their importance until for some reason we face being deprived of them. In the course of our average day, we hardly ever say that ''life'' is most important to us. Average days are composed of smaller things than life, things that in their own unobtrusive way fill us with joy and happiness, and that make the big Life worth living. Sure, we can keep heart patients alive, we can keep life going for them. But when we talk to people like Pat, we learn again how important the *quality* of that life must be. We learn that, as health care professionals, we have to attend to the daily lives of our patients, in addition to what we might do to cure their disease. We have to make it possible for them to return to the little things in life they really love. They must be able to come home in the evenings like Pat, who sits down with her husband and relaxes with an evening cocktail. They have to be able to come back in a year to the Arizona Heart Institute, look up the flight of stairs in our lobby and then . . . *run* them.

2 Knowing Your Heart

What will the Heart Test actually do?

The Heart Test will allow you to calculate your risk profile, that is, a profile of the major risk factors that produce atherosclerosis, the disease that many people refer to as "hardening of the arteries." Actually, atherosclerosis is a disease process that may begin in early childhood and continue throughout life. It is a clogging of the arteries that carry blood with its oxygen and nutrients to all parts of the body. Cholesterol, triglycerides, and other fatty substances build up to such a degree that the channel in the artery is too small to let sufficient blood pass through. If blood is cut off from nourishing the heart muscle itself, a heart attack can result. If blood to the brain is blocked, you can have a stroke. The Heart Test in this book will show you how likely the chances are of either of these happening to you. There are certain risk factors that indicate your chances. The Heart Test will show you where you are on the risk factor scale.

Risk Factors

The risk factors in heart disease may indicate to a great extent the current condition of your heart. A risk factor is a condition or a circumstance that affects the health of your heart by directly contributing to the development of atherosclerosis, which is the cause of heart and blood vessel disease. Some risk factors are modifiable, that is, you have the ability to change them by some intervention program. Other risk factors are not modifiable. The nonmodifiable risk factors are conditions that are beyond your control. These include your age, sex, family history, and your own previous medical history of heart attacks and strokes. These are all circumstances that you—and your heart—must live with.

Of equal or more importance are the modifiable ones, because with these you can intervene. With these you can take definite steps to modify your life-style to safeguard the health of your heart. The modifiable risk factors are blood fat levels, high blood pressure, overweight, diet, exercise, stress, smoking, and diabetes. It is probable that with additional research we will identify other factors sometime in the future, but as of now, these are the critical factors in heart disease.

You can learn, as did the hundreds of thousands of other Americans who watched the "20/20" program, what your most serious risk factors are and which ones can be altered and even eliminated. An advantage you will have, that the "20/20" program could not provide for the viewing audience, is that by the time you finish reading this book, you will know what steps you should take to maximize your cardiovascular health. Part II of this book deals exclusively with the modifiable risk factors and shows you how to handle each one, either to eliminate its deleterious effects upon your heart or to reduce those effects to a less harmful level of impact. You will understand how to implement the most up-to-date techniques in preventive medicine. You will learn to mobilize the health potential of your body and mind to insure your heart, as much as is humanly possible, against cardiovascular problems in the future. Just like the family who thew away their valentine candy, you will learn that good health and a good heart will demand some personal sacrifices.

It Works

We know our Heart Test works. A random sampling of people who took our test when it was first presented on television contacted us later to say that they became worried over their high scores and went to their doctors for checkups. In some cases, those with high scores discovered from further testing at heart clinics that they needed more intensive treatment. Some have since had open-heart surgery. If it had not been for our Heart Test on ABC, they might not be alive today. Other less fortunate viewers did not get medical help in time. Some of them did die. In the final chapter of this book we will share with you some of their stories in more detail.

But we were not satisfied with the random letters and cards that arrived slowly over the months since the "20/20" program in February. We decided to check for ourselves to see what degree of accuracy our Heart Test actually achieved. Was it a reliable instrument of testing or not? We wondered how people with already diagnosed cardiovascular disease would score if they took the test. So we took two hundred patients that we knew had serious atherosclerosis. Many had had heart attacks. Some were candidates for open-heart surgery. We administered the Heart Test to them to see if they would score in the high-risk end on our scale of twelve questions. They did. In each case, the patient's score placed him or her in the serious-risk category. They, too, had they taken the test earlier, could have predicted their chances of what now has befallen them. They could have known months ago, maybe even years ago, that they were likely candidates for cardiovascular disease. They might have sought out a program of preventive medicine to lower their risk factors and perhaps prevent the pain and suffering that each of them has gone through. In short, they could have known that they would be—as they now are—heart victims.

A Widespread Movement

Your heart keeps you alive, but are you keeping it alive? Most of us would have to answer honestly, "I really don't know." The average man and woman know so little about one of the most vital organs of the body. Since you can't see it, or really feel or hear it in the course of your day, you tend to ignore it. We all do. Or, I should say, those of us who pay little heed to the demands of our hearts tend to ignore them. Fortunately, not everyone falls into this category. A growing number of concerned Americans have made up their minds—and hearts—to prevent the number one killer in the United States, heart disease, from taking over another million lives this year. What is truly exciting for us in the health care profession is that over the last fifteen or twenty years a nationwide movement has sprung up among people like yourselves to fight cardiovascular diseases. The results of this movement are already being witnessed. The number of deaths from heart attacks and strokes has actually declined in recent decades. We are not sure exactly why. We do know that more people are learning ways to keep their hearts healthy and strong.

For example, many people have eliminated substantial amounts of fats, salt, and sugar from their diets. More Americans are exercising regularly, using especially the aerobic exercises that strengthen the heart and blood vessel system. Many have quit smoking. Countless numbers of people are taking stress-reduction courses, meditation seminars, biofeedback training, and many are learning Zen and yoga and a host of other methods, both ancient and modern, for leading calmer, more tranquil, less stressful lives. In some communities, a large percentage of the citizenry has completed CPR courses—cardiopulmonary resuscitation. When a member of their family, a co-worker, or a neighbor suffers a heart attack, these people know the split-second emergency techniques needed to keep the victim breathing and the heart beating until help can arrive. Lastly, the decline in cardiac-related deaths is undoubtedly due to the better care heart victims are receiving, the proliferation of heart clinics, better-trained medical technicians, improved surgical techniques, and the advances in technology used to screen and treat potential victims.

And still, heart disease continues to take more lives in America than any other disease. In fact, America leads the nations of the world in deaths from heart attacks. The only place that tops America in heart attacks is a remote area in northern Finland where coronary disease is in epidemic proportions. So even though deaths from coronary disease have declined in America, the battle against it is far from over. In some respects, it has only just begun.

A New Beginning

We are standing on the frontier of another new beginning that will advance the prevention of heart disease. Over the coming years, more Americans will take tests similar to the one in this book. Many will undergo the more extensive testing like the kind we do in our outpatient clinic in Arizona. This new breed of people will not be mystified by the "mysteries" of their hearts. These people will form the vanguard for reducing the heart risks that riddle our society and rob us of the quality of life we deserve. They will understand that to combat cardiovascular disease we need to study not only the disabled heart but the disabling society. To track down and eliminate the many sources of heart problems, we need to go outside our bodies and inspect the environments in which we live. We need to take a good hard look at our disabling life-styles. In one sense, your heart is not "at the heart" of the problem. Your heart is merely the target where the real problems thrust themselves, and sometimes when it is too late.

In terms of preventive medicine, the real problem is a holistic problem and what is called for is a holistic solution. Like working a jigsaw puzzle, you must take into account all the various pieces of your life in order to see the total picture. Indeed, to understand your heart better, you will need to know yourself better. You will need to do some serious thinking about your life because only with sound knowledge of who *you* are, and what *you* need, can you begin to acquire knowledge of your *heart* and what it needs.

So to begin, let's find out who you are, where you are starting from, and what circumstances about your life are beyond your control. To begin a total program of health care, you must accept some very basic facts about your life. For example, your age, sex, family bloodlines, and any previous heart attacks or strokes are already established. You can't really do much about them. They are a given, beyond your powers to alter. Let's face these facts squarely as unalterable risk factors because knowing what they are is the first step in developing your personal program toward preventing heart and blood vessel disease.

3 Who Are You?

How many times have we looked at photographs of ourselves and exclaimed, "Me? That doesn't look like me at all!" Even though our friends think it does, we aren't convinced. So we complain about how the camera caught us at an inopportune moment, and blame it on a slant of light, a distorting shadow, or the sun in our eyes. We all have difficulty in accepting certain things about ourselves, things we'd like to change or improve on if we could. Each of us is a composite of strengths and weaknesses, good points and bad points. No one is perfect or free from the little blemishes, scars, and quirks that are part of being human.

So it is with your heart. If you could see a photograph of your heart, you might exclaim, "That's it? Just that?" And you would know there was more to it than "just that." There must be. Your heart means more to you than just the organ that pumps blood throughout your body every minute of the day and night. For centuries, human beings have enshrined the heart as a symbol of much more than just a pumper of blood. It has been the seat of the emotions, of love and hate, passion and melancholy, the inner personality, the very core of life itself. Until just recently it has been intricately associated with the human soul, so that when a heart stopped, it was assumed the person was dead and the soul gone. Today, of course, we know that a heart can stop without causing death. We know that whatever the soul of life is, it does not flee the body just because the heart stops beating. With modern medical technology, we are able to stop the heart for a few hours at a time without losing life. On a heart-lung machine a patient can even have the heart removed and then replaced with another heart without disturbing the eternal soul. No, "who you are" transcends even the innermost core of your body—your human heart.

But there is no denying the vital importance of your heart and the role it plays in your own uniqueness. You are unique. You have a special history, a singular medical past, a configuration of events, people, and personality that produced your current state of health. If we could take your "medical mug shot," and hang it on a wall of a hospital along with others, you might be shocked. You might object to being hung in a rogues' gallery of the sick, the crippled, the cancerous, the suffering. You might say, "But I'm healthy and strong. Why put me there?" And we might answer. "Because of your heart. You can't see it, you can't feel or hear it, but it's malfunctioning. If you knew it better, you would understand." If you knew yourself—and your heart—better! Philosophers, sages, and poets have been giving that advice for centuries. And now doctors are advising you, "Know thyself. To thine own self be true."

The underlying philosophy of the Heart Test is that you *can* learn more about your heart and be true to it. Weather conditions may be beyond your control, but heart conditions are not. The condition of *your* heart—what you should think of as your "heart condition," even though this does not mean that you have any serious heart trouble—can be influenced by you. Whatever your "heart condition" is, you should be genuinely concerned about it. If you are not interested in something as important as your own health, then you must be like one of those rare and unfortunate people who can look at any photo of themselves and not care what the camera has done to them. When it comes to issues that involve your heart, it is impossible to say, "My heart's just not in it." Your heart *is* in it! And what life, or circumstances, or genes, or you yourself have done to your heart is significantly more important than what your friend's camera did to your image on film.

The Heart Test will help you acquire a personal sense of your own health. It will give you a profile of your "heart condition" and no matter how life has pulled at you or hauled you around in the past, you will be in control of the future. In short, you can and must take charge of your heart and its future. But first you must realize what elements of your life are *not* under your control. You must find out who the "nonmodifiable you" really is.

The Nonmodifiable Risk Factors

You can begin by realistically evaluating your nonmodifiable risk factors. Learn what limitations they may impose on you. Do not compare yourself with others. Forget their mug shots, their portraits, their own claims to strength or endurance. What is important is you.

Gender

If you are male, your chances of having heart disease are higher than if you are female. Until recently susceptibility to heart attacks and strokes has been almost a male prerogative, part of what it means "to be a man," along with soldiering, fathering, sporting, and ruling. But just as women have assumed their own positions in these areas in recent times—even "fathering" when a single mother needs to raise her children without a man in the household—so too have women begun to fall victim of heart disease. In the last few years, more women have been suffering heart attacks, and among men, heart attacks are occurring at earlier ages. I think these are the "changes of the seventies," and no doubt they will continue through the decade of the eighties. In fact, heart attack as a major killer is a twentieth-century phenomenon. It seems perversely planned that as the century draws to a close with our own generation, what began earlier in our parents' and grandparents' generations as a problem for older men will become commonplace for younger men, and even women.

Why are women today suffering from cardiovascular disease when their mothers and grandmothers before them were relatively free from it? No one knows for sure. It was assumed that the female hormone estrogen provided some kind of immunity to cardiovascular disease, since those few women who did have strokes or heart attacks had them after menopause. Estrogen may have prevented the development of atherosclerosis in women. We know that today more women have high-stress jobs and are smoking more than they did in their grandmothers' time. Both stress and smoking raise your chances of having heart problems. Many women are also less physically active in modern society, where convenient labor-saving devices eliminate the average housewife's need to exert very much physical energy doing the same jobs that her mother found to be backbreaking. In addition, even though the final word on the effects of oral contraceptives is not in, and won't be for years to come, it is evident that women who are on the pill have a tendency to retain more fluid in their bodies, which can lead to higher blood pressure. Both of these conditions can affect the heart adversely. It appears that one of the negative side effects of the women's movement has been to deny women their traditional freedom from heart disease.

Aging

Age is a peculiar thing. We are told to act our age, look our age, dress our age, and yet not many people agree on what all this means. Most of us would prefer *not* to look our age, since American culture puts such high value on youth and looking young. Supposedly, if you believe the media, the younger you look the better. Whatever the Pepsi Generation is, we are supposed to want to be part of it. It looks like fun, at least the commercials do. There was a time of course, somewhere in middle or late adolescence, when most of us wanted to look a little older in our rush into adulthood, or at least the pleasures and privileges of adulthood, if not the responsibilities. Driving a car, ordering a drink, sneaking into an R-rated movie—we couldn't wait. Now we can wait. It's those photos that make us look old that elicit our ardent denials that they look like us.

How old are you, anyway?

Your heart is older, you know. Not by much of course. But we never include those months of gestating in our mother's womb when we calculate our age. Your heart was beating then. You heart may outlive you, also. One of the ironic miracles of medical technology is that it can keep your heart beating long after your brain has died and your body retains very few signs of normal life.

Several years ago when heart transplants were more common than today, we invented a preservation chamber for hearts while working with Dr. Michael DeBakey at Baylor College of Medicine and Methodist Hospital in Houston, Texas. We were able to fly from Houston to another medical center, remove the heart and lungs from a donor, place them in the chamber, and fly by Lear jet back to Houston where they could be studied for potential transplant. Yes, it is possible for your own heart to go on beating just as it did in your mother's womb even after other vital signs of life, such as brain waves, have ceased.

But none of this means that your heart is a perennial fountain of youth. It ages along with you and grows old. You decline in cardiovascular efficiency, just as your strength and endurance in jogging or swimming or dancing wane also. Naturally, we all know exceptions to these so-called principles of aging. I've seen people in their sixties and seventies who continue to lead lives about as active as when they were in their thirties and forties. In fact, they seem indefatigable. Nothing slows them down. Perhaps from their own perspective, they are slowing down, going dancing only once a week instead of twice like they did when they were younger, or swimming only ten laps a day instead of the fifteen they used to do. It is possible to train yourself to stay active, much like an athlete who maintains his or her prowess beyond what are considered the peak years. Peak performance is as slippery a notion as aging.

No two people are alike. No two hearts are exactly alike. Yours is unique, and even though you know it will age along with you—and there is no reversing this as yet—you should not compare yourself with others, even people your own age. Get to know your own heart—and your own age—and live accordingly.

What this means is that you should not expect to retain the strength and endurance you had when you were young. Your blood vessels become less flexible, less elastic with age. Blood pressure tends to increase with age. Atherosclerosis, which can begin in childhood, may now be further advanced, making it even harder to get the same volume of blood through your arteries. So even though your chances of heart ailments are slightly greater as you age, you should not become overly worried by the fact that you and your heart are growing old. Aging is, after all, a normal, natural process.

If you must worry, worry about premature aging that has nothing to do with the number of years you have lived. Worry about what we call "accelerated atherosclerosis." We have found this condition in young people still in their twenties. We have even discovered people in their thirties who have needed bypass surgery—the grafting of a vein from the thigh to go around the blocked artery in the heart. You should guard against an overindulgent life-style that can wreak havoc on your body so that you age before your time.

Most people who develop atherosclerosis, however, do so slowly over the years. Atherosclerosis is a metabolic disease. The longer you live, the more likely the ramifications of this disease will become apparent.

Family

The last time you dug out that photograph of the family reunion, to share a few laughs and renew old memories, you were looking at a family portrait of heart disease. *Your* family portrait, because heart disease runs in families. If you were to ask me for the most foolproof protection against cardiovascular disease, I would have to answer glibly, "Pick your parents carefully." If in the time since the family reunion, or before it, for that matter, any of your close relatives—parents, grandparents, brothers, or sisters—had a heart attack or a stroke, your chances of having one are higher than if you had come from a family free of heart troubles. Studies of families, twins, and siblings have shown that the love song's request, "Make of our hearts, one heart," has some genetic truth to it. Members of families may share the same proclivities toward heart disease. In fact, data that have come in to us from the "20/20" program have now been analyzed with regard to family history as a risk factor. It is beginning to look as if a family history of heart disease may be one of the most important indicators of heart disease. Of all the people who scored High on the risk factor scale, 99.6 percent had a positive family history of heart disease. Of those who scored Medium, 90.4 percent had a positive family history. And of those who were in the Low category, only 16.9 percent had a positive family history.

Are these tendencies inherited by being passed down genetically from generation to generation? At this point, we don't have all the answers to that. It is possible that the level of lipoproteins in a person's blood is inherited. High-density lipoproteins (HDLs) are protein molecules that attach to fats in the blood and thus prevent them from being deposited in the arterial walls. Consequently, they have a protective influence that may reduce one's chances of developing serious atherosclerosis. If lipoproteins are genetically received from one's parents, then the heredity factor is a major determinant in the development of heart disease. Similarly, there are other metabolic processes we inherit from our parents that may influence either for or against atherosclerosis.

In addition to the inherited tendencies toward heart disease, there are environmental factors to consider. Some of these are modifiable, but we should consider them along with other family risk factors because, like them, they are part of our past, which is now beyond our control and which has partially produced the persons we are today. What you are today is partly a matter of genes and partly a matter of environment, a balance between nonmodifiable and modifiable risk factors. The old dichotomy of nature versus nurture applies to the causes of heart ailments just as it does to behavioral characteristics. You can, however, begin to alter the environmental conditions that are detrimental to your health. You do not need to continue to live "in your parents' house." What is more, you can begin to change the environment in which you are raising your own children, an environment that may have overwhelming influence in their chances of suffering from heart disease. What are some of these factors that you may be passing on to your children by your example and life-style?

Cholesterol levels, high blood pressure, and being overweight are closely related to stress, eating habits, exercise, and other patterns of daily living. Even what psychologists call Type A behavior, and we in the health care profession see so often in heart victims, can be learned at home. (We'll take a closer look at this uptight, harried, can't-seem-to-get-enough-done attitude that Type A's exhibit, in the chapter on stress. So, if *you* are Type A and are anxious to know more about it right now, *relax!* There's more to come.)

We have seen atherosclerosis in very young children. You might say that it is a "childhood disease" for many of us. The insidious thing about it is that it can go undetected for years, long into adulthood. Yes, the number one killer in America— heart disease—can be born and raised in comfortable, middle-class families across the nation. If you are exposing your own children to poor eating habits, you may be an unwitting accomplice to this "killer." Poor eating habits can lead to obesity, diabetes, a blood count high in fatty substances (cholesterol and triglycerides), and high blood pressure. A stressful homelife of quarreling, belittling, overdemanding parents, bitter sibling rivalries, financial insecurity, or whatever, may also be bad for the heart. Similarly, if you do not encourage your children to lead an active physical life with plenty of exercise, you lay the foundation for a lazy life-style for them later on when they are adults.

In short, if we could paint a portrait of the most likely candidate for heart disease, it would be someone overweight, overly compulsive, hypertensive (high blood pressure), with poor dietary habits and little or no exercise. There should also be a pack of cigarettes in the portrait. All of these, even smoking, can be learned at home.

Your Medical History

Santayana said, "Those who cannot remember the past are condemned to repeat it." Of course, he was speaking of history and governments. But the same might be said for your own personal histories as well, the pasts we all drag around with us, even though many of us reject them, or think we have. Like so many pioneers who settled out here in the great Southwest, we may want to leave our pasts behind to start life over. We don't like to think that we *cannot* start life over. It is part of the great American tradition to strike out for new beginnings. But in one sense, you can't. You can't completely escape your medical past, particularly if that past has included heart disease, a stroke, or surgery on your heart or blood vessel system. I don't mean to frighten you by saying that if you have suffered a heart attack in the past, you are doomed to repeat it. By no means! In fact, the whole rationale for this book is to convince you that you need *not* be a victim of your past, or your present, for that matter. However, it is still medically and statistically true that a major risk factor for having heart and blood vessel ailments in the future is that you have had them in the past.

First, let me caution you about what I *don't* mean. I don't mean angina—the heavy, squeezing pressure, often excruciating, that you may feel in your chest and arms on occasions when a coronary artery is not delivering enough blood to some area of your heart. It can occur when you are excited, overstressed, exerting yourself physically, as in exercising, doing yard jobs, or making love, and it usually lasts a few minutes and goes away when you stop the activity and rest. Even though it may feel like an elephant standing on your chest, and even though it is the most common symptom of heart attacks, angina is not necessarily a passport to a heart attack. Some people with atherosclerosis suffer angina and never have a heart attack. In fact, you may develop what we call "collateral circulation," additional arteries that will conduct blood around the one obstructed by plaque, the fatty buildup that narrows the artery with atherosclerosis. Also, you should not confuse the myriad pains and pressures that we all feel now and then in our chests with angina. There is a long litany, too long to recite here, of the one hundred and one causes of chest pain, everything from a touch of food poisoning to sleeping funny on your neck. I also don't mean congenital heart problems, like a hole in the septum or a pulmonary valve that won't open and close properly. These are no indication that you are destined for heart attacks or strokes.

No, the medical past that you cannot avoid is legitimate heart attack or stroke. These afflictions tend to recur, although having endured them in the past does not make it inevitable that you will have to go through them again. It merely means that if you have had a past history of heart problems like these, your chances of having them again are higher than those of someone who has never had them.

In summary, your present commitment to learning about your heart should not overlook your past experiences. In some sense, they hang around to haunt you and warn you about your risk of future heart troubles. They have produced the "nonmodifiable you." As a responsible human being, you need to take into account your entire self, as much of the totality of "who you are" as possible. You owe it to yourself to assess your chances for heart disease. Know who you are, where you are coming from, and where your heart is on the scale of both modifiable and nonmodifiable risk factors.

Where is your heart? I think we should consider the reverse of the wise saying in Scripture, "For where your treasure is, there will your heart be also." Rather, where your heart is, there is what you will treasure. And where is your heart? After centuries of myths, poems, and proverbs, after decades of research, experiments, and scientific breakthroughs, it is still at the vital center of "who you are."

4

The
Heart
Test

The Heart Test in this chapter may save your life.

It may prevent you from becoming one of the million people who will die of cardiovascular disease each year. After reading the next few pages and answering the twelve questions on the Heart Test, you will have rated your chances and calculated whether your overall risk is high or low. You will know the answer to the question that motivates many people to come to the Heart Institute in the first place: "Am I likely to become a victim of heart disease?" Based on a consideration of your risk factors and, if need be, other more sophisticated testing, we can rate your chances of it, and if your chances are high, we can prescribe the measures you must take to avoid becoming part of the statistics.

You already know something about your chances for developing heart disease from considering the nonmodifiable risk factors as you did in the previous chapter. Some of the basic aspects of *who you are* have been determined by them. Now you will place these factors alongside the modifiable ones and discover *where you are* on the conplete risk factor scale.

Read the following descriptions of the twelve risk factors and answer each of the questions as honestly as you can.

1. **Age:**

As you get older, your chances of suffering from heart disease increase. There is no preventing this general pattern. A man or woman past fifty-five years of age is more likely to have a heart attack or a stroke than a person younger than this. Age, then, is a nonmodifiable risk factor but not a very serious one. Therefore,

—if you are 56 or over .... score 1
—if you are 55 or younger .... score 0

2. **Gender:**

The way things currently stand, if you are male your risk of cardiovascular complications is greater than if you are female. Even though the occurrence of heart attacks among women is increasing for a variety of reasons that we have already considered in the previous chapter, we must still rank men as a higher risk than women. Therefore,

—if you are a male .... score 1
—if you are a female .... score 0

3. **Family History:**

Heart disease runs in families. So if you come from a family in which there is cardiovascular disease, your chances of getting it yourself are higher than those of someone whose family is free of it. Particularly telling is whether one or more of your close relatives—grandparents, parents, brothers, or sisters—suffered a heart attack or stroke before age 60. Therefore,

—for one or more close blood relatives who have had a heart attack or stroke at or before the age of 60 .... score 12
—for one or more close blood relatives with a known history of heart disease at or before age 60 but no heart attacks or strokes .... score 10
—for one or more who have had a heart attack or stroke *after* the age of 60 .... score 6
—otherwise .... score 0

4. Personal History:

If you already have a history of cardiovascular disease, your chances of continued problems with it are therefore greater than for someone who has never had heart trouble. Unfortunately, cardiovascular problems can be recurrent. Therefore, if you have a history of heart attack, stroke, cardiovascular surgery, or other arterial disease (not including varicose veins), you will have to consider yourself a greater risk. So,

—if you have had one or more at or before the age of 50: a heart attack, heart or blood vessel surgery, or a stroke .... score 20

—if you have had one or more after the age of 50 .... score 10

—if you have had none .... score 0

5. Diabetes:

There is a high frequency of cardiovascular disease among diabetics. If you know that you are a diabetic mark the statement that most closely resembles your own condition. If you have never had diabetes, score zero. Therefore,

—if you had diabetes before age 40 and are now on insulin .... score 10

—if you had diabetes at or after age 40 and are now on insulin or pills .... score 5

—if your diabetes is controlled by diet, or your diabetes began after age 55 .... score 3

—if you have never had diabetes .... score 0

6. Smoking:

You can pretty much guess that your risk level is going to increase dramatically if you are a smoker, more so if you smoke a lot, less if you smoke in moderation. Carbon monoxide in the bloodstream competes with oxygen for transport to the cells in the body, thereby reducing the amount of oxygen you have available for utilization in your body's cells. So, to counteract this effect, your heart has to work harder to supply oxygen to the cells. Carbon monoxide can damage the lining of your arterial blood vessels and increase the deposit of

materials that form atherosclerosis. Smoking also causes
vasoconstriction, that is, your blood vessels narrow when
you smoke. So if you are a smoker, get ready to add
points to your risk level. On the other hand, if you are a
reformed smoker, you'll get a break. Depending on how
long ago you kicked the habit, your risk level will be
less. Therefore,

—if you smoke two or more packs of cigarettes a
  day .... score 10
—if you smoke between one and two packs a day
  or quite smoking less than a year ago ... score 6
—if you smoke 6 or more cigars a day or inhale a
  pipe regularly .... score 6
—if you smoke less than one pack of cigarettes a day or quit smoking more than a year
  ago .... score 3
—if you smoke less than 6 cigars a day or do not
  inhale a pipe regularly .... score 3
—if you have never smoked .... score 0

7. Cholesterol:

If you know your cholesterol level, answer this question, and then skip question 8. If you do not know your
cholesterol level, skip this one and answer question 8.
So,

—if your cholesterol level is 276 or above ......
                                         score 10
—if it is between 225 and 275 .... score 5
—if it is 224 or below .... score 0

8. Diet:

I'll have a lot more to say about proper nutrition later.
For now, all you need to know is that if your diet is rich
in fat, especially cholesterol and saturated fat, you run a
greater risk of being troubled by heart disease. High
cholesterol and triglyceride (other fatty material) levels
in the blood often cause atherosclerotic deposits in the
lining of the arteries. As the deposits build up, the
arteries narrow, thereby impeding the flow of blood
through them. If the blood flow to the heart itself is
seriously cut off, a heart attack occurs. If blood flow to

the brain is reduced, a stroke results. So think about your diet and see how it matches the descriptions given below. Therefore,

—in your regular eating pattern if you have at least one serving of red meat daily, more than seven eggs a week, use butter, whole milk, and cheese daily .... score 8

—in your regular eating pattern if you eat red meat four to six times a week, eat four to seven eggs a week, use margarine, low-fat dairy products and some cheese .... score 4

—if you eat poultry, fish, and little or no red meat, three or fewer eggs a week, some margarine, skim milk, and skim milk products ... score 0

9. **High Blood Pressure:**
   There is a normal range for your blood pressure. When it goes above this range for a persistent length of time, you have what we call high blood pressure (hypertension), which causes your heart to pump with more force to get blood through your arterial system. It is an insidious disease because it can go undetected for a long period of time. There may be few symptoms, if any. It can strike you without warning. If your blood pressure is normal, your chances of heart trouble are lower. Therefore,

   —if *either* number in your blood pressure reading is 160 over 100 (160/100) or higher ...
   score 10
   —if *either* number is 140 over 90 (140/90) but less than 160 over 100 (160/100) .... score 5
   —if *both* numbers are *less than* 140 over 90 (140/90) .... score 0

10. **Weight:**
    Obesity is a serious health problem in this country. It also aggravates other conditions throughout your body. Later we will consider ways to achieve and maintain your ideal weight, but for now, figure out if you are overweight. The more extra pounds you carry around with you, the more you tip the scale in favor of suffering a heart attack later on.

Fill in the blanks to determine your ideal weight and if you are overweight.

Your height, _____ feet _____ inches, minus 5 feet = _____ inches over 5 feet.

Multiply inches over 5 feet, ⟶_____, by 5 pounds = _____ pounds per inch over 5 feet.

Add pounds per inch over 5 feet, ⟶_____, plus 110 pounds (men) or 100 pounds (women) = _____ pounds, ideal weight.

Subtract your ideal weight, _____ pounds, from your present weight, _____ pounds, = _____ pounds over-weight. So,

    —if you are at least 25 pounds overweight ......
                                        score 4
    —if you are 10 to 24 pounds overweight . score 2
    —if you are less than 10 pounds overweight ....
                                        score 0

11. Exercise:

Physical activity is good for you. Lack of it may aggravate heart problems. If you are in the habit of engaging in aerobic exercises that cause your heart rate to increase, such as jogging or swimming, you may be in much better shape to ward off future heart problems than someone who leads an excessively sedentary life and gets very little physical activity. Read the following descriptions of exercise routines and mark the one that most closely resembles your own. So,

    —if you engage in any aerobic exercise (brisk walking, jogging, bicycling, racketball, swimming) for more than 15 minutes less than once a week .... score 4
    —if you exercise that hard once or twice a week .
                                        score 2
    —if you engage in that exercise three or more times a week .... score 0

12. **Stress:**
    We have learned in recent years that certain personality types are more prone to cardiovascular disorders than others. Yes, your own personality and the way it influences your behavior and your perception of stressful situations can increase your chances for heart attacks. If you are one of those individuals who is unable to relax, who is constantly hurried and tense, never finding time to enjoy the gentler things of life, you are a more likely candidate for a heart condition than someone with the opposite characteristics and style of living. Therefore,

    —if you are frustrated when waiting in line, *often* in a hurry to complete work or keep appointments, *easily* angered, irritable . . . .
    score 4
    —if you are simply impatient when waiting, *occasionally* hurried, or *occasionally* moody . . . score 2
    —if you are relatively comfortable when waiting, *seldom* rushed, and easygoing . . . . score 0

Score Results:
    Now tabulate your points. Compare them with the chart below. Please remember that a high score does not mean you *will* develop heart disease. It is merely a guide to make you aware of a *potential risk*. Since no two people are alike, an exact prediction is impossible without further individualized testing.

With Answer to Question 9	Without Answer to Question 9
High Risk . . . . . 40 and above	High Risk . . . . . 36 and above
Medium Risk 20–39	Medium Risk 19–35
Low Risk . . . . . 19 and below	Low Risk . . . . . 18 and below

5   Now What?

How worried should you be now that you know what your risks for cardiovascular illness are? A little? A lot? It depends, of course, on just how serious a risk level you are at, how the odds of time, place, family, and living habits are stacked against you. But you need not succumb to the odds. You might say that you can buck the odds by taking the proper steps right now to reduce your risks.

Part II of this book is a program based on the methods we have been using at the Arizona Heart Institute to help people with your same configuration of risk factors to reduce those risks. Or if your risk level is now low, our program will help you keep that level low so that five, ten, or fifteen years from now you will not find yourself at a dangerously high position on the risk factor scale. What we tell the many people who come to us and write us at the Heart Institute we are now going to tell you. We will give you the latest developments in preventive medicine. Of course, if you scored in the high-risk range on the Heart Test, you should consult your doctor *immediately*. Our data indicate that high scores lead to serious trouble. The Heart Test does not provide a diagnosis; it only indicates your risk. Therefore, more precise evaluation should be gotten as soon as possible by using the latest technological testing methods that give a more accurate in-depth reading of your heart and blood vessel system.

Most people, however, unless they are in the high-risk category, can begin a preventive program like the one here. And, in fact, most people should. There is really no excuse for continuing ignorance about heart disease and its prevention. You have seen your risk factors. You will now learn what can be done about them. You know the relative importance of each one. For example, you have seen that your personal history of heart ailments and your family history of heart disease score very high. You also know that these are nonmodifiable risk factors. They should stand as constant warnings to you that something must be done about your other risk factors to lower your overall risk level. You know that smoking is a lethal habit. Our program will show you how to quit. If you have high blood fat levels, you should not continue to indulge yourself with meals rich in cholesterol and carbohydrates. Being overweight and lacking essential exercise habits rank lower on the risk scale, but they are both issues you can face and alter.

You may have already paid penalties for a careless, perhaps even reckless, life-style that is injurious to your heart. If you do nothing now, chances are that you will continue to pay those penalties in the years to come. Eventually it catches up with you. You may not think of your way of living as careless or reckless, but how frequently we are oblivious to the real damage we do ourselves, particularly our hearts. We certainly don't want to end up like the person who lived to a great old age but in such poor health that he said regretfully, "Had I known I was going to live so long I would have taken better care of my body." Sooner or later we realize what we are doing to ourselves, and by then it may be too late.

In a recent study octogenarians who were all in remarkably good health for their eighty-some years were asked to what they attributed their overall fine state of health. A common answer was that "Mother was right." What they meant was that staying fit can be achieved by commonsense practices similar to those our mothers taught us when we were young. Of course, some mothers give bad advice, but the point is that the best principles for long, healthy lives are natural, common, and should be able to fit into our normal daily living. Eat right, get plenty of exercise, sleep well at night, don't smoke, don't drink to excess, have an optimistic attitude.

Whether you are twenty, forty, or eighty, you are living within a margin of risk. Your job is to expand that margin by lowering the risks that are alterable. It can be done. It means a careful assessment of everything in your life that may figure in the cause of disease. Specific changes will be needed to set you on a course that is compatible with and not destructive of cardiovascular health. We think that, for the most part, you will see our recommendations as a variation on the "Mother was right" plan, rather than anything so farfetched and outlandish that you will think you are being asked to reshape your life into something that could exist only under the most artificially controlled and unnatural conditions. We don't anticipate putting you in a climatically controlled greenhouse for exotic cardiovascular specimens. Of course not. You will find our plan natural and comfortable once you have made the initial break with your old habits. Breaking with these old habits may seem impossible at first, but we will show you how it can be done. Living by the new ones will then be a breeze.

I hope that this Heart Test will be one of the major turning points in your life. I hope that from what you have learned about yourself you will zealously make a commitment to taking care of your heart. The attitude that "Well, we all have to go sometime, so why should I worry about it" is an old-fashioned one, considering the marvelous advances that have been made in preventive medicine and health care in recent years. It is true, of course, that there is some fate, destiny, or divine providence that keeps tabs on us. How to balance a fatalism that says "nothing can be done" with the old belief that God helps those who help themselves? I think an old Christian monk put it best when he advised that we should "Pray as if everything depended upon God, and work as if everything depended upon us."

So what I am asking of you is to take a "fix-it attitude" toward your life. You have bought fix-it books for other things that break apart, run down, need refurbishing. This book is a fix-it manual for your life-style so that your new way of living can prevent heart disease in the future. Any good fix-it manual should include preventive maintenance. Well, this handbook for your heart is your preventive maintenance plan. An optimism based on sound principles of preventive medicine can increase your chances of overcoming the disabling risk factors that you scored high on. We have seen this attitude work at the Institute. We know many patients who have shaped up their lives, and consequently their hearts. They are living healthier, stronger lives today because they determined to do so.

Let me give you a variation on the old motto, "Physician, heal thyself." *Patient,* heal thyself. What this should mean is that getting well—and staying well—is a joint effort on the part of both doctors and patients. People, like yourself, should have confidence in their innate, even intuitive, understanding of their health problems. You will still need a good doctor's advice, but a major component of health is the *desire* to be healthy. From my experience in heart surgery, I find that the patient who is rolled into the operating room with a strong desire to get well recovers more rapidly than those who lack that strong desire for normal, productive living. Just as a seriously ill patient needs the will to recover, so too do you need the will to *stay* healthy and *prevent* major illnesses from striking you.

A preventive program like ours requires you to remove the obstructions to good health. You are familiar with many of these obstructions by having taken the Heart Test. They include smoking, poor diet, lack of exercise, stress, high blood pressure, obesity. All these factors figure into your state of health. What you must keep in mind as you read the rest of this book is that the sum of all these things is greater than their parts. This is not mathematics, where that would not be true. This is humanmatics. The components of your life work synergistically, that is, they reinforce each other, intertwine, combine in ways you are not aware of. For example, being overweight makes exercising more difficult. It's hard to drag those extra pounds around in competition with lean, quick people whose excess baggage is at a minimum. Even walking tends to be slower among fat people than thin people. Many fat people will unconsciously overeat so that they stay fat and consequently do not have to compete with others in sports or exercise. If they are fat, no one will ask them to play tennis or go for a hike or walk down to the river, and, to them, that's good because it's too much trouble to do those things! And being overweight can raise your blood pressure. So you can see that obesity is not an atomistic condition, complete unto itself. It is part of a package of other conditions and attitudes, all of which contribute to heart disease.

What is required, therefore, and what we will show you, is a holistic approach that takes into account the many-faceted life you live. We will show you how *not* to compartmentalize your thinking about health, but rather how to view your state of health in terms of your total life-style.

Your mind, your body, your emotions—all interact with each other and contribute to overall well-being or overall ill-being. You must begin to look upon the many facets of your life—and especially your health—in their entirety, in their interrelatedness. Your outlook, your perspective is as much a factor in good health as diet, exercise, medicine, or therapy. John Milton put it, "The mind is its own place, and in itself can make a heav'n of hell, a hell of heav'n." Your attitude is that important, that crucial!

To increase your margin of good health so that you can live joyously and as safe as possible from cardiovascular disease, you must begin to see how your tennis shoes, your ashtray, your belt size, what you nibble on while you watch TV, the way you dash to answer the phone, what you do on a Saturday afternoon when you have nothing to do, and even the uncontrollable rage you'd like to direct at a poky waitress—all have in common. In the framework of cardiovascular health, these are all interrelated. They are all components that must be taken into account. None can be overlooked. The following chapters will show you how to evaluate these kaleidoscopic pieces that total up to be the health of your heart. Even if your risk scores were low in many of these areas, I would encourage you to read each of the sections on reducing risks anyway. We have found in our preventive medicine program that the advice and encouragement one patient gives to another is often the key to successful results. With the knowledge you gain in the following pages, you may be of assistance to a friend. Furthermore, you will be learning ways to keep your low risks in a safe range so that they do not later become high-risk factors for you.

Again, I hope your taking our Heart Test will be a turning point in your life, in the life of your heart. Only time will give you the answer as to whether *you* will be a victim of heart disease or not. But it is also time that can influence that answer. You have taken the time to complete the Heart Test, now *make* the time to adjust your life-style in ways that reduce your more serious risk factors.

I recently had an interesting conversation with Av Westin, the executive producer of the ABC News "20/20" show. He related to me that in the last year he has found the time in his hectic eighteen-hour-a-day schedule to run in Central Park or wherever

he might be traveling. Coupled with some prudent diet selections, the results has not only been loss of pounds, but more
importantly, a better ability to handle the high stress of his job.
In effect, he has *made* more productive time in his life by *taking*
the time to do something about the potential high risk of cardiovascular disease.

Too many people look upon time as the enemy, thinking that
eventually it is bound to catch up with them. But time is also our
friend and ally. Beginning today, you can initiate a new time in
your life, a time that might save your life and extend it into
many rich and rewarding years ahead.

PART II

Reducing Your Risks

Protecting your heart can be accomplished only by reducing the risk factors that threaten it. To reduce your risk factors you must make major changes in the way you live. There are no simpler cures, even though we might wish there were. A question I am frequently asked when I am lecturing about atherosclerosis is, "Doctor, can't I take some pill to dissolve all those cholesterol and fatty buildups in my arteries?" The answer is "NO." As of now, no one has invented a Drāno for humans. There is no drug, medicine, food, or exercise that can preserve the health of your heart by itself. Something as important as your heart requires greater care and attention than any one-shot cure-all could ever give it. It demands a total commitment to a healthier life. Heart care cannot be relegated to the weekend, like cutting the grass or playing a round of golf. Heart care is a way of living, an attitude about yourself that permeates your entire life. There is no minute in which your heart takes a break and leaves you stranded on your own, even though you might think so if you have ever experienced a skipped heartbeat or two. Similarly, there should be no laziness or indifference in your own efforts to care for your heart.

The next five chapters constitute your handbook for risk reduction. Here is a program that can prevent heart disease. In this section you will find the best methods for reducing the heart risks you scored high on in the Heart Test, the risk factors that create a portrait of your heart's true condition. You must attend to all of them in your heart-care program in order to safeguard your health. If the many pieces of your life do not work together to keep your heart healthy, they will work against each other, your heart suffering in the process. Remember that if your heart is presently disabled in any way by one or more risk factors, you must correct the disabling life-style that fosters and encourages those risk factors. Heart disabilities and the disabling risk factors do not exist in isolation or a vacuum. They are intimately woven into the way you live. If you want to continue to live an active and fulfilling life, you must institute for yourself a total program for risk reduction.

Don't wait until it is too late. Begin now. You can determine that your mode of living will ensure optimum good health. The following pages will show you the precise methods for modifying the menacing risk factors that threaten your life.

6 The Smoking Factor

After almost twenty years of warnings from the Surgeon General, 54 million Americans continue to smoke. The number of male smokers has declined about 15 percent since the first government report came out in 1964, but during that time more women have taken up the habit. The growing rate of smokers among teenage girls is alarming and shocking. Of all segments of the population, theirs includes the fastest-growing percentage of smokers.

In spite of these statistics, it has become increasingly less socially acceptable for men and women to smoke in public places. If this trend continues, the health of the nation should improve. More nonsmokers are asserting their right to clean, healthy air, and the managers of shops and stores across the country have requested smokers not to light up. "Air in use . . . no smoking please." Nonsmoking sections are springing up in more restaurants and movie theaters, and it seems like the smoking section in the back of airplanes gets smaller and smaller. At the Arizona Heart Institute building where there has never been a single cigarette lighted, the sign on the front door reads: "Smoking is a serious health hazard. Please honor our commitment to good health. No smoking on the premises.''

Nevertheless, what the Surgeon General calls the largest preventable cause of death in the United States, smoking, is still for many people a depressing and defeating fact of life. Sadly, many smokers assume that once they are hooked, that's it. Nothing can be done. They fatalistically accept themselves as ''smokers,'' brush aside warnings from friends, perhaps make a mental note to try quitting *sometime,* but not now, and light up another cigarette. And so the death statistics continue to climb. Among all the disease-related causes of death, the death rate for smokers is higher than for nonsmokers. Among middle-aged men who smoke, the death rate is three times that of nonsmokers. Furthermore, smokers are sick more often, contract more respiratory illnesses, miss more days of work, and have higher insurance rates. No wonder! There seems to be some inherent death wish in the life-style of smokers!

You would think that Nature's defense mechanisms against smoke in the lungs—the common cough, the irritating sensation in the chest, not to mention the watery eyes and burning in the nose—would convince us that smoke was not meant to penetrate the human body. To thwart Nature's warning signals by persisting in smoking suggests one thing: smoking is a *learned* behavior, an acquired habit. Smokers have twisted Nature's distress signals into pleasures, and have learned to ignore them. But I'm sure even heavy smokers would get Nature's point if they were trapped in a burning building and engulfed in smoke, just as nonsmokers get the point by sitting in someone else's smoke stream. In fact, ''side-stream smoking''—inhaling the smoke from the tip of someone's cigarette, pipe, or cigar—is a dangerous health hazard. Some studies show a greater concentration of carbon monoxide in smoke curling off the tip than in smoke inhaled through the cigarette.

No matter how you look at it, smoking is still as obnoxious, foul, and loathsome as it was when James I of England ranted against it while allowing his countrymen to colonize the area they called Virginia by planting . . . tobacco!

Smoking: "Real" Reasons and "Good" Reasons

If you are a smoker, I'm sure you have plenty of reasons for continuing to smoke. Most heavy smokers I've known have "real" reasons and "good" reasons for smoking. The "real" reasons are: they're hooked, they can't stop, it takes too much willpower. Things like that. They usually don't give me the "real" reasons. Instead, I hear the "good" ones. Excuses like "Well, I don't really smoke all that much. I used to smoke a lot. But not now. I've really cut down." What these people don't realize is that any amount of smoking is harmful. Here is another "good" reason: "Smoking is one of my few pleasures in life." It that's true, I feel sorry for those people who must rely on a deadly pleasure for lack of others. If it is really true that they have no other pleasures, they should do some hard self-evaluation about the way they live and find ways to get more pleasures into their lives. There are surely pleasures in life that involve fewer risks than smoking.

Some people refer to their cigarettes, cigars, and pipes as "my friend." Again, what a deadly friend! If you could extract the nicotine from five cigarettes and drink it, it would kill you in three minutes. Your so-called friend is one of nature's most lethal poisons. Nicotine makes a great insecticide. Your friendship with Old Nic would be a different matter if you had bugs in your lungs. Many pipe and cigar smokers brag that their method of smoking is safer because their tobacco is air-cured and hence the smoke is more alkaline and irritating and therefore difficult to inhale. They think they're safe because, as they frequently tell me, "We don't inhale the smoke like the cigarette smokers do." Foolishness! Watch them puff it in sometime! In addition, the lining of the mouth absorbs nicotine from pipe and cigar smoke to a greater degree than from cigarettes. All in all, it doesn't really matter. Smoke of any kind is dangerous to your heart.

Some people say that they are "only hurting themselves" and that they "have to die from something, anyway," so why not smoke? Why not? Two reasons. First, side-stream smoke does affect others, particularly children who must live in households with parents who smoke. A patient I recently saw who had been a bartender for many years was told by his doctor a few years ago that even though he didn't smoke, he had the lungs of a heavy smoker from inhaling the air in a smoky bar night after night. Second, even though you have to die someday, why speed up the process? As a smoker you run a higher risk of dying than a nonsmoker.

Similarly, don't let the family legends about Aunt Flora and Uncle Fauna who "smoked a pack a day and lived to be a hundred" fool you. Some people are lucky, and even though they may have lived to a ripe old age, it does not mean they lived healthy lives to that age. The age might have been ripe, but their health could have been rotten. Remember also, risk factors are additive. If you smoke and have other risk factors, the final score may lead to your final countdown.

If you scored high on the cholesterol or hypertension questions on the Heart Test, smoking will be a compounding risk factor. In addition to the damage it can do your body independently of other factors, as a sole cause for heart and respiratory ailments, smoking works synergistically as an accomplice to these other two. We see over and over again in our screening labs that smokers who have high cholesterol levels and have high blood pressure run substantially higher risks in contracting coronary heart disease. Some merely suffer from it. *Some* die.

How Does Smoking Damage Your Health?

People frequently ask me that. I wish the answer were simple to give. But it's complicated. First, the carbon monoxide decreases the amount of oxygen in your blood. Both carbon monoxide and oxygen compete to become part of the red blood cells that carry oxygen through the body. It may seem that Nature is perverse in this instance, but carbon monoxide actually has a greater affinity for red blood cells than oxygen does. So when you smoke, your blood is less oxygen-rich and your entire body suffers because of it. Also, your bone marrow overreacts and produces extra red blood cells to compensate for the ones locked up with carbon monoxide. This, in turn, thickens your blood. Your heart naturally finds it more difficult to pump thicker blood through your body. To make matters worse, nicotine constricts the blood vessels, so the heart has to pump harder to deliver blood to the body, blood that is already less effective in nourishing your cells. With your blood vessels constricted, the pressure upon the walls of the arteries is greater and thus your blood pressure goes up.

In addition, smoke in the lungs causes the small hairs called cilia, that move gently and rhythmically sweeping dust and germs from the lungs, to slow down their sweeping action. This makes them less effective in keeping your lungs clean. Eventually, these cilia will disappear. That's why smokers have more respiratory problems than nonsmokers. Also, with smoke in the lungs, the natural flow of blood and oxygen is altered, causing the oxygen exchange to be less effective.

Why Do You Smoke?

If you smoke, you can begin to eliminate this risk factor in heart disease by scoring yourself on this "Why Do You Smoke?" test developed by the federal government.*

Here are some statements made by people to describe what they get out of smoking cigarettes. How *often* do you feel this way when smoking them? Circle one number for each statement.

Important: Answer every question.

	always	fre-quently	occa-sionally	seldom	never
A. I smoke cigarettes in order to keep myself from slowing down.	5	4	3	2	1
B. Handling a cigarette is part of the enjoyment of smoking it.	5	4	3	2	1
C. Smoking cigarettes is pleasant and relaxing.	5	4	3	2	1
D. I light up a cigarette when I feel angry about something.	5	4	3	2	1

*U.S. Department of Health and Human Services Publication No. (PHS) 80-50120.

	always	fre-quently	occa-sionally	seldom	never
E. When I have run out of cigarettes I find it almost unbearable until I can get them.	5	4	3	2	1
F. I smoke cigarettes automatically without even being aware of it.	5	4	3	2	1
G. I smoke cigarettes to stimulate me, to perk myself up.	5	4	3	2	1
H. Part of the enjoyment of smoking a cigarette comes from the steps I take to light up.	5	4	3	2	1
I. I find cigarettes pleasurable.	5	4	3	2	1
J. When I feel uncomfortable or upset about something, I light up a cigarette.	5	4	3	2	1
K. I am very much aware of the fact when I am not smoking a cigarette.	5	4	3	2	1
L. I light up a cigarette without realizing I still have one burning in the ashtray.	5	4	3	2	1
M. I smoke cigarettes to give me a "lift."	5	4	3	2	1
N. When I smoke a cigarette, part of the enjoyment is watching the smoke as I exhale it.	5	4	3	2	1
O. I want a cigarette most when I am comfortable and relaxed.	5	4	3	2	1
P. When I feel "blue" or want to take my mind off cares and worries, I smoke cigarettes.	5	4	3	2	1

	always	fre-quently	occa-sionally	seldom	never
Q. I get a real gnawing hunger for a cigarette when I haven't smoked for a while.	5	4	3	2	1
R. I've found a cigarette in my mouth and didn't re-member putting it there.	5	4	3	2	1

How to Score:

1. Enter the numbers you have circled to the test questions in the spaces below, putting the number you have circled to Question A over line A, to Question B over line B, etc.
2. Total the three scores on each line to get your totals. For example, the sum of your scores over lines A, G, and M gives you your score on *Stimulation*—lines B, H, and N give the score on *Handling,* etc.

Totals

_____ + _____ + _____ = _____
 A   G   M   *Stimulation*

_____ + _____ + _____ = _____
 B   H   N   *Handling*

_____ + _____ + _____ = _____
 C   I   O   *Pleasurable Relaxation*

_____ + _____ + _____ = _____
 D   J   P   *Crutch: Tension Reduction*

_____ + _____ + _____ = _____
 E   K   Q   *Craving: Psychological Addiction*

_____ + _____ + _____ = _____
 F   L   R   *Habit*

Scores can vary from 3 to 15. Any score 11 and above is *high*; any score 7 and below is *low*. Learn from Score Analysis what your scores mean.

Score Analysis

What kind of smoker are you? What do you get out of smoking? What does it do for you? This test is designed to provide you with a score on each of six factors that describe many people's smoking. Your smoking may be well characterized by only one of these factors, or by a combination of factors. In any event, this test will help you identify what you use smoking for and what kind of satisfaction you think you get from smoking.

The six factors measured by this test describe one or another way of experiencing or managing certain kinds of feelings. Three of these feeling-states represent the *positive* feelings people get from smoking: (1) a sense of increased energy or *stimulation*, (2) the satisfaction of *handling* or manipulating things, and (3) the enhancing of *pleasurable feelings* accompanying a state of well-being. The fourth is the *decreasing of negative feelings* by reducing a state of tension or feelings of anxiety, anger, shame, etc. The fifth is a complex pattern of increasing and decreasing "craving" for a cigarette representing a psychological *addiction* to cigarettes. The sixth is *habit* smoking that takes place in an absence of feeling—purely automatic smoking.

A score of 11 or above on any factor indicates that this factor is an important source of satisfaction for you. The higher your score (15 is the highest), the more important a particular factor is in your smoking and the more useful the discussion of that factor can be in your attempt to quit.

A few words of warning: If you give up smoking, you may have to learn to get along without the satisfactions that smoking gives you. Either that, or you will have to find some more acceptable way of getting this satisfaction. In either case, you need to know just what it is you get out of smoking before you can decide whether to forego the satisfactions it gives you or to find another way to achieve them.

Stimulation

If you score high or fairly high on this factor, it means that you are one of those smokers who are stimulated by the cigarette— you feel that it helps wake you up, organize your energies, and keep you going. If you try to give up smoking, you may want to safely substitute a *brisk walk* or moderate exercise, for example, whenever you feel the urge to smoke.

Handling

Handling things can be satisfying, but there are many ways to keep your hands busy without lighting up or playing with a cigarette. Why not toy with a pen or pencil? Or try doodling. Or play with a coin, a piece of jewelry, or some other harmless object.

There are plastic cigarettes to play with, or you might even use a real cigarette if you can trust yourself not to light it.

Accentuation of Pleasure—Pleasurable Relaxation

It is not always easy to find out whether you use the cigarette to feel *good*, that is, get real, honest pleasure out of smoking (Factor 3) or to keep from feeling so *bad* (Factor 4). About two-thirds of smokers score high or fairly high on *accentuation of pleasure*, and about half of those also score as high or higher on *reduction of negative feelings*.

Those who do get real pleasure out of smoking often find that an honest consideration of the harmful effects of their habit is enough to help them quit. They substitute eating, drinking, social activities, and physical activities—within reasonable bounds—and find they do not seriously miss their cigarettes.

Reduction of Negative Feelings, or "Crutch"

Many smokers use the cigarette as a kind of crutch in moments of stress or discomfort, and on occasion it may work; the cigarette is sometimes used as a tranquilizer. But the heavy smoker, the person who tries to handle severe personal problems by smoking many times a day, is apt to discover that cigarettes do not help him deal with his problems effectively.

When it comes to quitting, this kind of smoker may find it easy to stop when everything is going well, but may be tempted to start again in a time of crisis. Again, physical exertion, eating, drinking, or social activity—in moderation—may serve as useful substitutes for cigarettes, even in times of tension. The choice of a substitute depends on what will achieve the same effect without having any appreciable risk.

"Craving" or Psychological Addiction

Quitting smoking is difficult for the person who scores high on this factor, that of *psychological addiction*. For him, the craving for the next cigarette begins to build up the moment he puts one out, so tapering off is not likely to work. He must go "cold turkey."

It may be helpful for him to smoke more than usual for a day or two, so that the taste for cigarettes is spoiled, and then isolate himself completely from cigarettes until the craving is gone. Giving up cigarettes may be so difficult and cause so much discomfort that once he does quit, he will find it easy to resist the temptation to go back to smoking because he knows that someday he will have to go through the same agony again.

Habit

This kind of smoker is no longer getting much satisfaction from his cigarettes. He just lights them frequently without even realizing he is doing so. He may find it easy to quit and stay off if he can break the habit patterns he has built up. Cutting down gradually may be quite effective, if there is a change in the way the cigarettes are smoked and the conditions under which they are smoked. The key to success is becoming *aware* of each cigarette you smoke. This can be done by asking yourself, "Do I really want this cigarette?" You may be surprised at how many you do not want.

Summary

If you do not score high on any of the six factors, chances are that you do not smoke very much or have not been smoking for very many years. If so, giving up smoking—and staying off—should be easy.

If you score high on several categories, you apparently get several kinds of satisfaction from smoking and will have to find several solutions. Certain combinations of scores may indicate that giving up smoking will be especially difficult. Those who score high on both Factor 4 and Factor 5, *reduction of negative feelings* and *craving*, may have a particularly hard time in going off smoking and in staying off. However, there are ways to do it; many smokers represented by this combination have been able to quit.

Others who score high on Factors 4 and 5 may find it useful to change their patterns of smoking and cut down at the same time. They can try to smoke fewer cigarettes, smoke them only halfway down, use low-tar-and-nicotine cigarettes, and inhale less often and less deeply. After several months of this temporary solution, they may find it easier to stop completely.

You must make two important decisions: (1) whether to try to do without the satisfactions you get from smoking or find an appropriate, less hazardous substitute, and (2) whether to try to cut out cigarettes all at once, or taper off.

Your scores should guide you in making both of these decisions.

Kicking the Habit

Many people would like to stop smoking. Some do. A small percentage of those who do—never smoke again. But the sad fact is that many who stop do start up again. It seems some people make a career or a hobby of kicking the habit! They've tried all the programs and eagerly await the newest. Most of the stop-smoking programs, however, claim only a 30 percent success rate. Even hypnosis has a rather small percentage of successes. One patient in our smoking program has had six heart attacks and has been in six different quit-smoking programs. He's back for another.

If you want to quit smoking, take this "Do You Want to Change Your Smoking Habits?" quiz, so you'll know what kind of motivation is behind your desire to quit.*

*US Department of Health and Human Services Publication No. (PHS) 80-50120.

DO YOU WANT TO CHANGE YOUR SMOKING HABITS?

For each statement, circle the number that most accurately indicates how you feel. For example, if you completely agree with the statement, circle 4, if you agree somewhat, circle 3, etc.

Important: Answer every question.

	completely agree	somewhat agree	somewhat disagree	completely disagree
A. Cigarette smoking might give me a serious illness.	4	3	2	1
B. My cigarette smoking sets a bad example for others.	4	3	2	1
C. I find cigarette smoking to be a messy kind of habit.	4	3	2	1
D. Controlling my cigarette smoking is a challenge to me.	4	3	2	1
E. Smoking causes shortness of breath.	4	3	2	1
F. If I quit smoking cigarettes it might influence others to stop.	4	3	2	1
G. Cigarettes cause damage to clothing and other personal property.	4	3	2	1
H. Quitting smoking would show that I have willpower.	4	3	2	1
I. My cigarette smoking will have a harmful effect on my health.	4	3	2	1
J. My cigarette smoking influences others close to me to take up or continue smoking.	4	3	2	1

	completely agree	somewhat agree	somewhat disagree	completely disagree
K. If I quit smoking, my sense of taste or smell would improve.	4	3	2	1
L. I do not like the idea of feeling dependent on smoking.	4	3	2	1

How to Score:

1. Enter the numbers you have circled to the test questions in the spaces below, putting the number you have circled to Question A over line A, to Question B over line B, etc.
2. Total the three scores across on each line to get your totals. For example, the sum of your scores over lines A, E, and I gives you your score on *Health*—lines B, F, and J give the score on *Example*, etc.

                                           Totals

_____ + _____ + _____ = _____

  A   E   I   Health

_____ + _____ + _____ = _____

  B   F   J   Example

_____ + _____ + _____ = _____

  C   G   K   Esthetics

_____ + _____ + _____ = _____

  D   H   L   Mastery

Scores can vary from 3 to 12. Any score 9 and above is *high*; any score 6 and below is *low*. Learn from the following section what your scores mean.

Score Analysis

Why do you want to quit smoking? Are your reasons strong enough for you to make the effort to quit? Do you have enough reasons? This is something only you can decide.

Four common reasons for wanting to quit smoking cigarettes

are: concern over the effects on *health*; desire to set an *example* for others; recognition of the unpleasant aspects (the *esthetics*) of smoking; and desire to exercise *self-control*.

This test was designed to measure the importance of each of these reasons to you. The higher your score on any category, say *health*, the more important that reason is to you. A score of 9 or above in one of these categories indicates that this is one of the most important reasons why you may want to quit.

Health

Research during the past ten or fifteen years has shown that cigarette smoking can be harmful to health. Knowing this, many people have recently stopped smoking and many others are considering it. If your score on the *health* factor is 9 or above, the health hazards of smoking may be enough to make you want to quit now.

Example

Some people stop smoking because they want to set a good example for others. Parents do it to make it easier for their children to resist starting to smoke; doctors do it to influence their patients; teachers want to help their students; sports stars want to set an example for their young fans; husbands want to influence their wives, and vice versa.

Such examples are an important influence on our behavior. Research shows that almost twice as many high school students smoke if both parents are smokers compared to those whose parents are nonsmokers or former smokers.

If your score is low (6 or less), it may mean that you are not interested in giving up smoking in order to set an example for others. Perhaps you do not appreciate how important your example could be.

Esthetics (the Unpleasant Aspects)

People who score high, that is, 9 or above, in this category recognize and are disturbed by some of the unpleasant aspects of smoking. The smell of stale smoke on their clothing, bad breath, and stains on their fingers and teeth might be reason enough to consider breaking the habit.

Mastery (Self-control)

If you score 9 or above on this factor, you are bothered by the knowledge that you cannot control your desire to smoke. You are not your own master. Awareness of this challenge to your self-control may make you want to quit.

Summary

This test has measured your attitude toward four of the most common reasons why people want to quit smoking. Consider those that are important to you. Even if none are important, you still may have a highly personal reason for wanting to change your habit. All in all, you may now see that you have reasons enough to want to quit smoking.

How to Pick a Program

Take an "all-or-nothing" attitude. There is a regular smorgasbord of programs utilizing a wide range of behavior modification techniques to get you to quit smoking. Directors of these programs admit quite candidly that the single most significant factor in whether or not a person will be in the 30 percent success group is *motivation.* You have to *want* to stop smoking. You have to become almost obsessed by the idea that you can lead a life free from cigarettes. To be a nonsmoker must displace other values you associate with smoking. In short, "to quit smoking" must become part of your belief system, almost like a religion. If you don't take this "all-or-nothing" attitude, your chances of quitting successfully in any program, no matter how fancy, are greatly diminished.

Look for small groups. At the Arizona Heart Institute we unite the group approach with the individualized method. How? By limiting the groups to no more than three or four people. A person trying to quit needs the support of others and yet needs personalized attention as well. We feel that small groups under the supervision of a quit-smoking therapist provide a dedicated participant with the best of both programs. He or she gets personalized attention from the counselor as well as mutual support from fellow members in the program.

Pick a program you like. There are many to choose from. Enroll in one that you think fits your personality, your time schedule, your way of doing things, and in which you have confidence. But always remember that it is merely your *tool* to quit smoking. It is not a surefire cure. *You* are the cure—your desire to quit. The mechanics of the program won't really matter that much. You'll make it work because you *want* it to.

A Home Program for You

Here is an abbreviated version of the method we use at the Arizona Heart Institute. You can use this method on your own to quit smoking, but we suggest you find a friend or two to join you. You will need the encouragement and support of others.

Your Baseline Stimuli Record

Prepare for yourself what we call a "Baseline Stimuli Record." For several days keep a log of the times, places, events, and people with whom you smoke. Analyze your smoking patterns and note the times, places, events, and people that most increase your desire to smoke. These are the situations you should work on first. These are your most frequent smoking stimuli that probably make you a habitual smoker. Remember that smoking is a behavior, not a curse, a learned behavior that springs from an urge. Something in your life, some favorite activity, place, or situation provides the stimuli for you to reach for a cigarette. When you have a pretty clear picture of your smoking pattern, and know where the stimuli are, the next step is to ambush your hand movement before you end up holding a cigarette. You can do this by making an active effort to change the triggering stimuli. For example, if you smoke at the table every time you finish a meal, you can begin to break up the smoking response chain by getting away from the table as soon as you take your last bite.

Your Urge-Reduction Statement Card

Once you have broken the smoking response chain, you may continue to have *urges* to smoke. A way to block these urges and prevent your reaching for another cigarette is to use an Urge-

AHI QUIT-SMOKING PROGRAM BASELINE STIMULI RECORD

DATE: _____

Time	Place (Where)	Event (What)	With Whom

Reduction Statement Card. Perhaps this will sound too easy to you or like some kind of gimmick. Well, it *is* easy and it is a *gimmick*! But it works, if you want it to. Here's what to put on your card:

Challenge Reminder. Recognize that urges are challenges just like other challenges you've met before in life. Think of a few challenges or urges that you successfully denied in the past, and how you denied them, and how proud you were of yourself for having done so. Write one on your card.

Now remember that you have a success already for denying urges, and the urge to smoke is just another urge that you can beat.

So when you get an urge to smoke, physically *stop* all activity. Next, make a simple statement to yourself like, "I have beaten other challenges in the past successfully and I can beat this challenge. I won't give in to this urge to smoke." Say this once to yourself.

Positive Reward. Next write a statement about some positive reward or benefit you will derive by beating this urge. Your reward may be something like you'll smell better and be more attractive to your date tonight who doesn't like the smell of tobacco on your breath.

Negative Consequence. Then pair this positive-benefit statement with a negative-consequence statement that will occur should you give in to your urge and smoke. The penalty for not beating the urge might be that other people in line will cast dirty looks at you or that your boss will be displeased or you will deaden your tastebuds right before you want to try a new recipe.

It doesn't matter what your positive and negative statements are. Make them something meaningful to you on each occasion you reach for your card. The more immediate you make them the better. Rewards like "I will live longer" and "I will have so much more money at the end of the month" are too distant to have immediate impact on the urge tempting you at the moment. So make them short-term benefits and penalties, and they'll work more effectively.

Ambush the Urge

Whenever you experience the urge to smoke a cigarette, pull out the card and keep repeating the three urge-reduction statements over and over to yourself until the urge goes away. When it does, congratulate yourself, for you have beaten it! That time. Be ready for the next urge. When it comes, stop *all* activity, and keep repeating your three statements until the urge goes away. Our experience with patients at the Heart Institute is that within two weeks smoking urges will diminish and then plateau out.

AHI QUIT-SMOKING PROGRAM URGE-REDUCTION STATEMENTS CARD

CHALLENGE STATEMENT:

1. This urge is a challenge like other challenges I have met and won before. I can and will win this one.
Challenges met: _____
_____

POSITIVE-REWARD STATEMENT:

2. The benefit I will gain from beating this urge is: _____
_____

NEGATIVE-CONSEQUENCE STATEMENT:

3. The penalty I'll experience for not beating this urge is: _____
_____

Repeat this series of statements whenever you desire a cigarette.

Charting Your Success

It also helps if you keep a success chart while learning how to beat your urges. Keeping track of your victories over cigarettes provides the encouragement you need to keep at it. The very process of chart-keeping reinforces your commitment to your goal. (Ben Franklin boasted that this was true when he was charting his daily success at acquiring thirteen virtues, although he admitted that he didn't do very well with humility!) So make a grid of the days of the month across the bottom and number of cigarettes smoked up the left-hand side and plot your progress. You'll be amazed at how the graph line will begin to plunge.

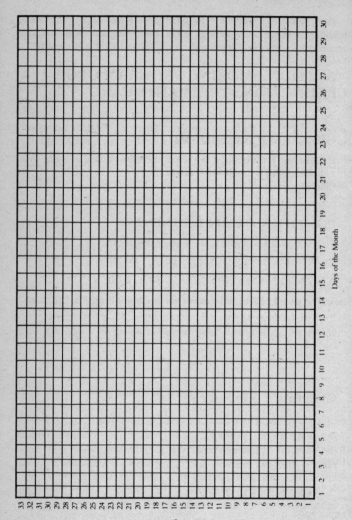

After you have quit smoking, make a similar chart with the number of *urges* along the left-hand side, instead of cigarettes, and chart your successes with these. Eventually, you'll see even your urges disappear.

Changes: What to Expect

As you quit smoking, you'll notice a number of changes in yourself. Some of these will be the obviously good ones that you were anticipating, like being able to breathe more easily, coughing less, having a better taste in your mouth when you wake up in the morning. You'll get less winded when you run or climb stairs. However, there may be some side effects you hadn't counted on.

Weight gain. You may gain a little weight, and if you're not careful, you may gain a lot of weight. If you notice a weight gain, you will have to take immediate corrective measures. The reason for this is that many people substitute food for cigarettes when their tastebuds begin to quiver for a cigarette. One oral need is substituted for another. Food will begin to taste better soon, too, because your mouth is cleaner and less deadened from smoke. For these reasons, many quitters experience a hearty and refreshed appetite. If you begin to gain weight, watch your diet, and exercise. Finding some exercise to do will cut down on the weight gain. You could begin our weight-management program explained in chapter 8 to supplement your nonsmoking program. Besides, now that you have quit smoking, exercising will be more enjoyable.

Nervousness. You may feel a little nervous in social situations because your old habit of smoking was one of those social crutches that put you at ease in front of other people. Now you're on your own. So don't worry if you should feel anxious, because something is missing from your usual routine. Something *is* missing—your former anxiety reducer. Be prepared to have what psychologists call a little "unresolved anxiety." You can find a less dangerous crutch than cigarettes if you really need something to do with your hands and mouth. Learn relaxation or stress-reduction techniques. Suck on a straw or fiddle with a pencil. Chew on a low-calorie cinnamon stick.

Smoking is one of the most serious risk factors in heart disease. You may remember that a heavy smoker had to score ten points on the Heart Test. You should take every means to eliminate smoking from your life. By itself, as a solitary agent, it places a host of disabilities upon your heart and respiratory system. In conjunction with high blood pressure and high cholesterol levels, it is a deadly accomplice to the strains they have already put upon your heart.

The
Stress
Factor

A few years ago, during the era of cardiac transplantation, I was in a group of cardiovascular surgeons sitting around having an informal conversation. Dr. Christiaan Barnard, the first surgeon to perform a human heart transplant, was among us and a reporter, spotting him, immediately moved into our circle and started to fire questions at him. The first was, "How much tension were you under the first time you took a human heart from one patient and sewed it into another?" "None," replied Christiaan. The reporter was shocked. "Do you mean to say you never have stress?" he inquired. "Of course I do," the surgeon replied. "When a blood vessel bursts, like a main water line in the street, and I have no way to control it. That is stress!"

Dr. Barnard hit on the key ingredient in stress—the situation in which we perceive our loss of control or one in which we never had control. Unfortunately, life by its very nature is full of uncontrollable situations for each of us. There is no such thing as "stress-free" life. Very definitely, stress is a risk factor in heart disease, but since there are proven methods of reducing

stress, it becomes one of the modifiable risk factors. We should
know, therefore, what we mean by the term *stress* and to what
extent stress can be modified, if not completely eliminated.

What Is Stress?

We like to associate stress with certain life-wrenching situations like the death of a close friend, getting fired, being di-
vorced, as well as the more humorous ones like spilling soup on
your hostess's dress, forgetting a business associate's name, or
riding three stops past your own on the bus. We often think of
certain high-pressure jobs as being stressful, like those of Wall
Street brokers, inner-city high school teachers, air-traffic controllers, and heart surgeons. Actually we would do well to shift our
thinking a bit and consider the fact that stress might not be in
either *situations* or *jobs* but in *ourselves,* in the way we perceive
and then respond to those situations and tasks.

Why?

First of all, these situations have built-in frustrations, and
frustration is an important component of stress. Usually it is the
frustration of not knowing what to do, not knowing how to gain
control of the predicament. Not all stress frustrations produce
negative responses in us. For example, the following could be
classified as stressful, but they are certainly not harmful; in fact,
some of them are fun: reading a spy thriller, watching a scary
movie, playing a ruthless game of poker, or being left cliff-
hanging on Friday when your favorite soap opera tunes off for
the weekend. When you think about it, you can actually enjoy
these activities, since the stress response is in no way deleterious
to your health.

Second, many people who we would think are engaged in
nerve-racking professions actually have the attitude of the artist
for whom work and play are almost indistinguishable. If you ask
artists what they enjoy doing most, the answer will most likely
be "paint." In other words, painting is, at the same time, work
and fun, like play. Many Wall Street brokers and business
tycoons, whose daily life pattern would look hectic and exhaust-
ing to us—filled with deadlines, last-minute changes, decisions
on which millions of dollars ride—may think what they do is sort
of fun. On the other hand, a barber cutting hair in his quiet shop
may perceive himself as in a pressure-cooker job and wish he

could hurry up and get done so that he could go home and putter around in the garden. The barber is under stress.

Third, when things do go wrong, much depends on whether or not we perceive the frustration as a challenge. It's like being lost on a side road and not being able to locate yourself on the map. Some people would panic and curse the highway engineers or cartographers, while others would look upon it as an adventure, a challenge that might provide unexpected excitement along the way. Our lives are filled with hurdles. Some people spring exuberantly across them. Others grudgingly strain to budge them out of the way. To these people there is no frustration at all.

Stress occurs when we are frustrated by a perceived obstacle blocking one of our desired goals. It is usually a feeling of helplessness in removing that obstacle. In such circumstances, we feel threatened and out "gut" reaction is either "fight or flight." So why don't we? Because we are civilized and mature. In more barbaric times, earlier on the calendar of evolution, we probably would have turned tail and run or clenched our fists, bared our fangs, and snarled violently. Occasionally, we can indulge in this primitive behavior without too much social disapproval from others. Haven't you kieked a candy machine that stole your money? Or have you just given up, walked away, and tried to forget it? Both reactions are not very satisfying and they don't produce your candy. But stress situations are like that. There is no easy solution, and we cannot really react violently or live comfortably with ourselves if we flee it.

Dr. Hans Selye, a pioneer in stress studies, has described the typical reaction of people locked in a stressful situation. First, they register alarm, an initial shock that what is happening is really happening. And to *them*! Then there are unsuccessful attempts to resist the situation. Whatever they try to do, they realize it won't work. Finally, exhausted by all this, they realize there is no emotionally satisfying way out of their predicament. During this sequence of events we say that a person is under stress that is harmful psychologically and physically.

Are there any clues that you are under stress? Yes. Psychologists who have studied thousands of people who suffer from stress have noted that certain physical and behavioral characteristics often accompany stress. Here is an inventory of the more common ones. You can check to see how many of them you tend

to exhibit when stressed. The list is not exhaustive, nor should
you think that every time one or more of these clues arises you
are in a dangerous "stress zone."

Stress Indicators

Stress may sometimes cause the symptoms listed below. Other
problems may cause them also, so they are not foolproof evidence that you are under abnormal stress. Nevertheless, it is
good for you to know what might be an indication that you are
under stress.

Increased smoking, or chain-smoking
Increased sweating
Headache, dizziness
Dry mouth or throat
Irritability or bad temper
Lethargy or inability to work
Cold, clammy, or clenched hands
Sudden bursts of energy
Finger-tapping, foot-tapping, pencil-tapping
Fatigue
Pacing
Frowning; wrinkling forehead
Restlessness
Rapid walking
Rapid speech
Muscular aches (especially neck, shoulders, back, or legs)
Increased appetite or loss of appetite (or overeating and not
    eating)
Inability to sleep, or nightmares
Desire to cry, or crying
Fear, panic, or anxiety
Coughing
Excessive snacking
Nagging
Unnecessary hand-waving, making wild gestures
Continuous talking
Nervous tic
Stuttering
Nausea or stomach pain

Grinding teeth
Low-grade infections
Rash or acne (especially on face or back)
Constipation or diarrhea
Frigidity or impotence
Loss of sex drive
High blood pressure
Depression
Hives
Withdrawal

Stress and Your Heart

What happens to your heart when you are under daily emotional stress, and what can you do about it?

At first, your endocrine system allows you to produce extra hormones. This is Nature's primitive way of getting you ready for the ordeal. Your heart responds to these hormones, especially adrenaline, by beating faster, since again, in more primitive times, your reaction would have required more blood and oxygen to either fight or run. This in turn increases your blood pressure, but not harmfully if it is for a brief period of time. However, it is dangerous if it remains at a high level because you are under continual stress. Sometimes stress can lead to arrhythmias—abnormal beating patterns of your heart—and possibly even to heart attacks.

So what can you do? Well, you can't avoid stress entirely. Occasionally you hear of people whose lives were too stressful, so they chucked everything and went to live on an island in the Pacific or in a farmhouse in New England. Did they beat the stress with these adventurous moves? Not really. Every life-style has some stress woven through it, even in Tahiti and Vermont. True, there are groups of people, and alternate ways of living, in which stress seems to be a negligible factor in heart disease, but you will have to travel far from modern life in the Western world to find them. Researchers have found relatively stress-free people among Somali camel herdsmen, Navajo Indians, certain orders of monks (the contemplative ones, not those with Ph.D.s who teach at high-powered universities), and average Yugoslavian peasants. Their life-styles don't sound too inviting. Would their life-styles work for you? Most likely not. It seems these groups of people, along with similar exotic populations in other parts of the world, show very little problem with stress but not solely because their pace of life is slower. They also display a ready acceptance of their cultures and have a sense of belonging to a supportive community to soften those moments in life that we, under other circumstances, would find stressful. So don't run off to Tahiti or Somalia.

Nevertheless, stress is not a monster in your life gone berserk. You can handle it. There are time-tested methods for reducing stress with which you can "de-stress" your life to a great extent. First, let's find out how stressed or de-stressed you are. You should have some idea of the stressors in your life and how you respond to them.

Fill out the following five inventories and score yourself on the Stress Profile chart. Here you will see the actual breakdown of why you may have scored high on certain questions related to stress on the Heart Test. When you have finished this, the rest of this chapter will give you practical, easy-to-understand suggestions for reducing stress.

Stress Cues List

Check items that occur frequently or often.

EMOTIONAL-COGNITIVE CUES:

I become overexcited _____

I worry _____

I feel insecure _____

I have difficulty sleeping at night _____

I become easily confused or forgetful _____

I cry easily _____

I think about several things at once _____

I become easily irritable _____

I become very uncomfortable or ill at ease _____

I become nervous _____

        Total Emotional-Cognitive Cues _____

PHYSICAL CUES:

I sweat profusely/hands get clammy _____

My face becomes "hot" _____

I shake or wiggle my feet when I sit _____

STRESS PROFILE

	29				
	28				
	27				
	26				
	25				
	24				
	23				
	22				
	21				
	20				
	19				
	18				
	17				
	16				
	15				
	14				
	13				
	12				
	11				
	10				
	9				
	8				
	7				
	6				
	5				
	4				
	3				
	2				
	1				
	0				
Cues	Type A Behavior	Relaxation	Thinking	Time Use	

I have frequent headaches _____
My muscles become tense or stiff _____
I feel my heart pounding _____
I have difficulty saying what I want to say _____
My stomach becomes upset or cramped _____
I have diarrhea or have colitis _____
I have twitches _____
Total Physical Cues _____

BEHAVIORAL CUES:

I act impulsively _____

I walk rapidly _____

I eat when I'm nervous or bored _____

I smoke when I'm nervous _____

I drink to make me less nervous _____

I often do two things at once _____

I work later than others _____

I'm more responsible than others _____

I am more competitive than others _____

I am frequently late or rushing to be on time _____

Total Behavioral Cues _____

Sum of Three Scores _____

TYPE A BEHAVIOR INVENTORY

The following statements are similar to those associated with Type A behavior. Circle the appropriate letter for each question.

	Fre-quently	Some-times	Never
1. Do you have problems getting along with your superiors at work?	F	S	N
2. Do you bring work home more than once a week?	F	S	N
3. Do you consider yourself keenly competitive or hard-driving at work?	F	S	N
4. Do you feel uncomfortable or upset when you have to wait in a long line?	F	S	N
5. Do you eat rapidly?	F	S	N
6. Do you generally prefer to do things yourself rather than have others do them for you?	F	S	N

7. Do you engage in two things at once, i.e., reading the newspaper while eating?   F   S   N

8. Are you easily irritated?   F   S   N

9. Do you become upset when others observe you while you are working on a task?   F   S   N

10. Do you go back to your work during your time off?   F   S   N

11. Do you try harder than most at what you do?   F   S   N

12. Do you feel like hurrying someone who takes too long to come to the point?   F   S   N

13. Do you generally walk faster during the day than you would if you were walking on a beach?   F   S   N

14. Do you believe yourself to be more responsible than others around you?   F   S   N

15. Do you think about other things when someone is talking to you?   F   S   N

SCORING:

Number of "F" answers _____ × 2 = _____

Number of "S" answers _____ × 1 = _____

Number of "N" answers _____ × 0 = _____

Add these three for a total of _____

RELAXATION SCALE

Put a checkmark in the column that most accurately answers each question.

	Frequently	Sometimes	Never
1. Do you take regular naps or relaxation breaks at least once per day?	_____	_____	_____

	Fre-quently	Some-times	Never

2. Do you plan "alone time" for yourself to engage in some pleasant activity at least once a day?

3. Do you regularly engage in some play activity?

4. Do you spend some time regularly in which you concentrate fully on only one task for an extended period of time?

5. Do you wear clothing that fits well and you feel good in?

6. Do you plan or organize your day's activities ahead of time?

7. Are you able to effectively "come down" at the end of the day in order to fall quickly asleep?

8. Do you actively attempt to create regular changes in your environment, i.e., take different routes to and from work, do routine tasks in different rooms, etc.?

9. Do you regularly monitor your tension behavior and take steps to reduce it, i.e., sit back in your chair and take several deep breaths, slow down your walking pace?

10. Do you engage in some exercise activity at least twenty minutes daily?

11. Do you allow time for yourself to daydream about your goals and future plans?

	Fre-quently	Some-times	Never
12. When worried do you know how to put troublesome thoughts into perspective to reduce their potency?	_____	_____	_____
13. Do you regularly spend time planning vacations and entertainment activity?	_____	_____	_____
14. Do you actively seek out humor in your life and spend some time laughing every day?	_____	_____	_____
15. Do you frequently act and respond in a spontaneous manner rather than in a controlled and calculated fashion?	_____	_____	_____

SCORING:

Number of "F" answers _____ × 2 = _____
Number of "S" answers _____ × 1 = _____
Number of "N" answers _____ × 0 = _____
Add these three for a total of _____

STRESS THINKING SCALE

Put a checkmark in the column that most accurately answers each question.

	Fre-quently	Some-times	Never
1. Polyphasic Thinking: Do you think of several things at a time, or find it difficult to concentrate on or persist with a thought to its completion?	_____	_____	_____
2. Low Self-Confidence: Do you think about yourself in depre-	_____	_____	_____

	Fre-quently	Some-times	Never

ciating terms or make negative
self-statements?

3. **Excessive Responsibility:** Do
you think of yourself as being
the only one or the best one
capable of carrying the burden
of completing tasks or projects?

4. **Self-Reference:** Do you think
predominantly in "I" terms
with you at the center of attention; i.e., do the words "I" or
"me" occur frequently in your
language and thoughts?

5. **Confusion:** Do you become
easily confused?

6. **Catastrophizing:** Do you think
of the worst possible outcomes
for unfortunate events or circumstances?

7. **Dichotomous Thinking:** Do
you think of things as being either one extreme or another;
i.e., good or bad, right or
wrong, best or worst?

8. **Negativistic Thinking:** Do you
think badly of events or circumstances or hold negative
thoughts about people?

9. **Angry Thinking:** Do you think
about things or people in your
past, the present, or the future
that generate anger or revenge
in you?

10. **Hypochondriacal Thinking:** Do _____ _____ _____
    you concern yourself or worry
    about your body or your health?

SCORING:

Number of "F" answers _____ × 3 = _____
Number of "S" answers _____ × 1.5 = _____
Number of "N" answers _____ × 0 = _____
                        Add these three for a total of _____

TIME USE SCALE

Circle the appropriate letter for each question.

	Fre-quently	Some-times	Never
1. Do you put things off until the last minute?	F	S	N
2. Would others consider you, or do you feel, harried or rushed?	F	S	N
3. Do you feel that you have made the best use of your time after completing an activity?	F	S	N
4. Do you plan your activities ahead of time?	F	S	N
5. Are you successful at ending time-consuming events easily, such as telephone calls, meetings, conversations, or activities?	F	S	N
6. Do you tell others beforehand how much time you have allotted for what you are about to do?	F	S	N
7. Are you an accurate judge of the amount of time an activity will take?	F	S	N

	Fre- quently	Some- times	Never
8. Do you plan for yourself a certain amount of "alone time" every day?	F	S	N
9. Do you plan time to be with others who are helpful or are willing to give to you?	F	S	N
10. Do you delegate tasks to others easily?	F	S	N

SCORING:

Number of "F" answers _____ × 3   = _____
Number of "S" answers _____ × 1.5 = _____
Number of "N" answers _____ × 0   = _____

Add these three for a total of _____

RELAXATION

Stress is more than just bodily tension but often it is accompanied by tightness, achiness, numbness, crampy feelings in different parts of the body. Just as you cause yourself stress, you cause the tension in your body. Conversely, since *you* do it, *you* can undo it. Throughout the centuries people have known the art of relaxation. I should say "arts" because there are many methods and techniques to relax. Since our modern life-style triggers a great deal of stress in people, it has become fashionable, even trendy or faddish, in recent years to take relaxation courses. Unfortunately, some people pay a lot of money to learn some very basic, natural, commonsense tricks to let their body go loose. For, actually, that is what your body is telling you when you feel tense. "Let me go loose!" You should know several relaxation techniques, since at different times and under different stressful contexts you may need to use the one that is most appropriate. Then, too, some people respond well to certain ones but not to others. Try several and use the ones that work for you. Remember, these are exercises, just like those in calisthenics or music lessions. You may not be skilled in them at first, but practice will make you better.

Moving Slowly

Moving slowly is very relaxing.

Sit comfortably and spread your fingers until they are as far apart as they will go. Do this slowly and experience each movement. Shift your concentration to your fingers and try to "become" one with the stretching movement in your hand.

Roll your head and rotate your feet and hands.

Hunch your back up and slowly let it sink back down into whatever position it wants to go.

Stand comfortably relaxed and slowly rise your arms up at your sides until they are at shoulder height. Let them feel light and airy and then slowly lower them to your sides.

The important point in all these exercises is to focus your attention on the slowness of your movements. Let your mind slow down as well. Clear it of all other thoughts except how good that part of your body feels where there is slow, gentle movement.

Relaxation Phrases

If you sit or lie down and listen to a gentle, soothing voice suggest relaxation, you will relax. Many people put relaxation phrases on tape and play them after they come home from work or school. If you know them you can say them to yourself without the bother of a tape. Say them slowly and pause thirty or forty seconds between each one. Focus your attention on the part of your body mentioned in the phrase that you are hearing.

I feel quite quiet.
I am beginning to feel quite relaxed.
My feet feel heavy and relaxed.
My ankles, my knees, and my hips feel heavy, relaxed, and
 comfortable.

My hands, my arms, and my shoulders feel heavy, relaxed, and
   comfortable.
My neck, my jaws, and my forehead feel relaxed.
My whole body feels loose and relaxed.
I am quite relaxed.

Of course, you can vary them or work on just one area of your
body at a time instead of these particular groups. It also helps to
imagine you are in some favorite, relaxing place, like a beach or
a picnic spot, a mountaintop, a chapel, or garden, before you
begin. Spend a few minutes with your eyes closed, picturing to
yourself what it looks like, seeing the colors and shapes, the time
of day, the light, feeling the air, imagining the smells and all the
sensory components of your place.

   There are several breathing exercises that can help us relax.
Here are a few you might find enjoyable.

Breath-Counting Exercise

   Do this two or three times a day for about five minutes each
time. You should be in a quiet, private place where you are
undisturbed. It helps to lie or sit comfortably. Inhale completely.
Take a good, full, slow breath while counting slowly to yourself.
See how many counts it takes. Then exhale just as slowly while
counting to the same number. You should not be counting higher
than about 4–6, and you should not be taking more than about
four breaths each minute. In other words, slow your breathing
down, make it rhythmical, let it relax you. Do this for fifteen
minutes. When you finish you will feel relaxed. It may not seem
like it to you at first, but you will actually get better at this with
practice. Stay with it for a week and you will find that each
time it relaxes you more quickly and easily.

Touching Your Breathing

   Touching is stimulating and relaxing. In this exercise, lie
down and breathe slowly and deeply. Think about your body as
it touches the floor or mattress. Next think about your breathing
for a few minutes. Watch how you breathe. Your breathing may
change a bit as you attend to it, but that's all right. Just observe
it calmly. Then put the palms of your hands on your chest so that

your hands do not touch each other and let them lie there for about sixty seconds while you feel your chest rise and fall to your breaths. Then put your hands down at your sides and experience whatever you feel in your chest, in your hands, in your entire body. Next, place your hands on your stomach above the navel for sixty seconds and experience the rise and fall there as you breathe. Again put your hands at your sides while you focus on the experience. Lastly, put your palms on your lower belly inside your hipbones and repeat the exercise. Always be aware of what you are feeling throughout this exercise. Always keep your breathing slow and rhythmical and deep.

Alternate Nostril Breathing

This exercise has been practiced in India for centuries and has recently come to the West with the renewed interest in yoga. Use your thumb and forefinger. Focus on your breathing. Close off your left nostril with your thumb and inhale through the right nostril. Breathe in slowly. Then close your right nostril with your forefinger and exhale through your left nostril. Then inhale through your left nostril and exhale through your right. Repeat from six to eight times. Do not hold your breath. Keep your eyes closed throughout the exercise and sit somewhere comfortable.

Faulty Thinking

In addition to our inability to relax, stress can be caused by the way we misperceive reality. We call this faulty thinking. What is faulty thinking?

Faulty thinking arises partly from the thoughts and images that are always present in our minds. We are constantly talking to ourselves subvocally, in our inner ear, reporting to ourselves the events of the present moment, criticizing, evaluating, making judgments. Sometimes we even form words with our lips, and become embarrassed when someone notices. I don't mean that we are as distracted as the bag ladies downtown who roam the streets with five shopping bags, two winter coats, and never stop their ceaseless chatter with themselves. No, we are quite sane even though we constantly engage in little running dialogues with ourselves, private conversations in which we try to explain the world to ourselves and make sense of things. This self-talk is a perfectly human process. But if we do not "report" events to ourselves accurately, we can slip into faulty thinking.

We want to investigate especially the ways that faulty thinking makes life stressful. Even though there are modern psychological theories to elucidate this process, wise people through the ages have recognized the truth of it. For example, in the first century A.D. Epictetus put it in a nutshell: "Men [and of course he meant women too] are disturbed not by things, but by the views which they take of them." In other words, it is not so much an event, but our *interpretation* of it, that causes our emotional reaction. The determining factor is the interpretation you make, and frequently you may not even be aware that you are "interpreting" at all. You might notice an event and think to yourself that *it* has caused you stress. You aren't aware of the in-between stage called "interpreting." It is this interpreting that produces your emotional disturbance.

Here's an example. Let's say that the current object of your affections breaks the news to you that he or she is going to start seeing someone else and would therefore like to cool it with you. You may think that your immediate reaction would be depression or maybe even hostility. But even though your emotional response seems to be split-second, there was an in-between step you overlooked: interpreting—the way you interpreted the news to yourself. You may have viewed yourself as a worthless person or unjustifiably jilted. Or maybe you had a glimpse of yourself as never being able to find another lover as nice as this one. Perhaps you saw the world as unfair and threatening to you. Maybe you thought of yourself as cheated. The important point is that if you viewed your situation irrationally, you jumped to extreme conclusions about yourself without good evidence. If you did not look at the sequence of events from alternative viewpoints, you may have created undue stress for yourself.

How else could you have interpreted the event? Could you have interpreted it more rationally or logically? You might have salvaged your ego a bit by reminding yourself that just because one person dumps you, it does not mean that you are a worthless person. Evidence is that other people have loved you. You might have considered other reasons for your friend wanting to see someone else. There might be evidence that there is some justification for it. If you interpreted your plight more *rationally*, you would most likely realize that your chances of finding someone else in life are pretty good. You won't have to spend the rest of your days alone, unwanted, unloved. Instead of blaming the problem on the whole world being unfair, you certainly have evidence of times when the world, or life, did not cheat you and treat you unfairly.

You see what can happen if you calmly and rationally study that split-second activity called "interpreting"? You might come up with more rational conclusions, conclusions that lead to a less stressful response. Naturally, you are still going to feel bad. It's appropriate. After all, it would be inhuman not to feel bad when a loved one leaves you, for whatever reason. But you may not end up totally depressed or hostile. Your emotional state will be sadness, perhaps, or annoyance, both easier emotions to handle, less stressful. Like the Stoics, for whom Epictetus was a chief exponent, you'll learn to react to upsetting events more calmly, more tranquilly. But don't expect to squash your emotions completely. Not even the Stoics did that. You need your emotions to be a complete human being.

The old suspicion that the emotions reside in the heart has some medical truth to it. Certainly emotions, especially those pumping adrenaline, can stir up your heart and increase the number of heartbeats. Irrational thinking can "overdose" your heart with adrenaline and produce stress. You don't need to be icy cold and unfeeling, though. Just scale down your reactions from white hot to lukewarm, and you'll be doing your heart a favor by interpreting events more rationally.

Albert Ellis, an early developer of cognitive psychotherapy, has put together a list of ten irrational ideas that often blur our interpreting process. How many of them distort *your* thinking about events? Which ones color your interpretations? You can use these irrational ideas as cues in your daily life that you may be engaging in faulty thinking and creating unnecessary stress for yourself.*

Irrational Idea No. 1: The idea that it is a dire necessity for an adult human being to be loved or approved by virtually every significant other person in his community.

Irrational Idea No. 2: The idea that one should be thoroughly competent, adequate, and achieving in all possible respects if one is to consider oneself worthwhile.

*From Albert Ellis, *Humanistic Psychotherapy* (New York: McGraw-Hill, 1973), pp. 242–43.

Irrational Idea No. 3: The idea that certain people are bad, wicked, or villainous and that they should be severely blamed and punished for their villainy.

Irrational Idea No. 4: The idea that it is awful and catastrophic when things are not the way one would very much like them to be.

Irrational Idea No. 5: The idea that human unhappiness is externally caused and that people have little or no ability to control their sorrows and disturbances.

Irrational Idea No. 6: The idea that if something is or may be dangerous or fearsome one should be terribly concerned about it and should keep dwelling on the possibility of its occurring.

Irrational Idea No. 7: The idea that it is easier to avoid than to face certain life difficulties and self-responsibilities.

Irrational Idea No. 8: The idea that one should be dependent on others and need someone stronger than oneself on whom to rely.

Irrational Idea No. 9: The idea that one's past history is an all-important determiner of one's present behavior and that because something once strongly affected one's life, it should indefinitely have a similar effect.

Irrational Idea No. 10: The idea that there is invariably a right, precise, and perfect solution to human problems and that it is catastrophic if this perfect solution is not found.

How to Reframe Your Thoughts

Many people suffer stress because of faulty thinking and they need to reframe their thoughts. This is a modification of the techniques we just spoke about. Thoughts are like pictures in a frame. If you mount them in certain frames, they don't do the pictures justice. Some frames are so imposing that the pictures get lost. Other pictures need large, ornate frames to bring out their special qualities. So, too, with thoughts. Put your thoughts about your experiences into the right mental frames and you'll see them for what they really are.

Here are some of the misassembled frames we stick our thoughts in and what to do about them.

The Global, Nondimensional Frame

People who think in a global, nondimensional framework see their experiences, and usually themselves, in extremely large, worldwide, sometimes cosmic dimensions. The following are global words: extremely, exceedingly, incredibly, awfully. When you think realistically about some of the statements they occur in, you might laugh. After all, how many things are really incredible or extreme? Here are some typical stress-filled comments:

I am extremely anxious.
I am awfully upset.
I am incredibly frustrated.

What can you do about statements like these? Put them into multidimensional terms that describe the situation more locally. Such as

I am somewhat anxious.
I am rather upset right now.
This problem is really frustrating.

Stop and think about yourself for a moment. Most often you are moderately upset or wishing things were different. Seldom are you pushed to the extremes that global statements indicate. When you hear yourself making one of these global, non-dimensional statements, stop and restate the experience in a more local, multidimensional way.

The Absolutistic, Moralistic Frame

Statements that are absolute and moralistic have two potential problems with them. Many times what you are talking about is not absolute. There are variations on it. And oftentimes the situation is not really a moral one, that is, it has very little or nothing to do with right and wrong. An absolute, never-changing attitude is not very realistic. We know, if we stop to think about it, that life is not always made up of clear-cut rights and wrongs. Frequently, situations are shades of gray, rather than black and white. As Robert Frost put it, "Most of the change we think we see in life is due to truths being in and out of favor." Life does change, even some things we once thought to be eternally true. Here are some misleading absolutistic, moralistic statements:

I am a horrible nervous wreck.
I have always been bad that way.
I always do the wrong thing.

Here are those statements, reworded to suggest what is probably closer to the truth:

I get nervous now and then, but so do other people.
Sometimes I act that way, even though I know I shouldn't.
Everybody makes mistakes once in a while.

Notice how these statements do not seem to be written in stone. Nor do they make a moral judgment about yourself.

The Irreversible Frame

Very similar to the absolute and moral frame is the irreversible frame. The supposition here is that nothing can be done about you or your way of handling stressful situations. Statements like these illustrate this framework:

I am basically prone to stress.
It's in my nature to fly off the handle.
That's just the kind of guy I am.

Why not take a reversible attitude? After all, most of the things that you tell yourself are irreversible might be the very ones you could reverse. In fact, many of them might be easily reversible with a little practice. Try saying

I can learn ways to handle stress.
I don't always have to give in to my so-called nature.
Is that the *only* kind of guy I am?

The Character Diagnosis Frame

This frame always makes us analyze our character rather than our behavior. Remember that your personality and your actions are two separate things. For example, when you reprimand a small child for spilling his milk by saying, "You're a bad boy," the child may eventually begin to think that you, who know so much more than he does, is right, that he is a basically bad person. Even with something like his hitting his little sister, it should be pointed out that what he *did* was bad, not he himself. If you point out to him that what he did was bad, then he can work on controlling his bad actions and not grow up with a warped sense of himself as some evil person. The same holds for you. Don't say to yourself

I am so lazy.
I am such an embarrassment.

Instead, focus your criticism on your behavior rather than your character. Say

I acted rather lazy today.
Sometimes I do embarrassing things.

You can find other faulty frames on the Stress Thinking Scale you filled out earlier in this chapter. Low Self-Confidence, Excessive Responsibility, Self-Reference, Catastrophizing, Dichotomous Thinking, and Negativistic Thinking are all frames that may warp the thoughts you put in them. When you think in these frameworks, you are bound to undergo stress because you are attempting to live in a reality that does not really exist, not the way you perceive it.

Anger

When you get angry, adrenaline flows, your muscles tighten, your heart beats faster, and your blood pressure rises. You are under stress. These are all typical stress reactions. As in other stress-inducing situations, your normal reaction is "fight or flight." You may want to lash out verbally at the person or problem that stirs your anger. You may want to harm someone physically. Anger is a frequent and all-too-common response to frustration.

Since you have been taught from childhood that you should *not* be violent and that you should control your anger, your civilized response may be to deny or repress your anger. In other words, you may turn it inward on yourself. Doing so may seem appropriate in society's eyes, but you have not alleviated the stress. Inward anger is still threatening, still stressful. You may even feel guilty, depressed, or weak and incompetent for having repressed the anger.

Heart attack victims and people who have had surgery frequently feel anger. Something has been purloined from their lives. They may have to slow down their activities, stay home from work, give up sports and hobbies for a while, remain in a hospital for an undisclosed length of time. Understandably they feel cheated, frustrated, and may get angry at life or God for having "done" this to them. You may even harbor a moderate degree of this kind of anger when you discover in the Heart Test that your risk factors are high. Anger arises from feeling helpless in the face of threats that appear too overwhelming for us to handle. Most people don't like to feel helpless or weak. It is demeaning to be caught in a situation that looks hopeless and defeating. Our normal reaction is to want to triumph, not go down in defeat. If we recognize our strengths and have confidence that we can survive what threatens us, we usually do not respond with anger. Instead we react from a position of power in a manner that can still express our annoyance and displeasure, but not as uncontrollable rage. Don't mistake appropriate, healthy displeasure for anger. There are, after all, a lot of things in life to be displeased about.

But if you cannot completely dispel your anger, you can reduce the intensity of it so that the stress will be less. You can do this tactfully without displacing your anger by hurting an innocent person or animal. There are more psychologically healthy ways to deal with anger than by coming home and kicking the cat or taking it out on your spouse or children. Anger can be expressed in safe, nonthreatening ways. Here are some you might try.

Uncorking your anger: Don't keep your anger bottled up. Uncork it. But do it calmly and rationally no matter how riled up you are. Force yourself to tell the other party that you are angry. The key here is to make your "anger statement" begin with the word "I." Say, "I am angry at you" or "I feel angry right now about what is happening" or "I am really mad." Beginning your statement with "I" puts you at the center of it, where you should be because it's *your* anger. Not someone else's. You make yourself angry over problems that arise. If you think of it this way, rather than think of other people and situations making you angry, you will realize you have much more control over your anger. And control is what you want because it gives you a sense of power to counteract the feeling of helplessness that triggers anger. So say it: "I feel angry." It's okay to feel angry.

Measuring your anger: You've been angry before. Remember the time when . . . ? Or that really awful time when . . . ? Or remember the time you were so angry, as you had never *ever* been, and you . . . ? Fill in the blanks. We've all experienced so many moments of anger in our lives, we should be able to rate them. Yes, make your own personal "anger scale" of incidents from your past, so that when new anger springs up, you will be able to gauge your response appropriately to your past history of anger. So if your son wrecks the car, you'll know that similar incidents made you "furious." Dropping something heavy on your toe is "maddening." Getting stuck in a traffic jam or a line that won't move is "annoying." A mosquito in your bedroom is "irritating." If you know at what level your anger is, you'll know much better what to do with it, how to express it, how to calm yourself down.

Looking beneath your anger: Sometimes anger is like a fallen log in the woods and you suspect there is a snake under it. But when you roll the log back, the snake isn't there. Think of anger as so many fallen logs across your path. When you stop to look under them and ask yourself *why* you are angry, or what will you lose, or what difference does it make, you may discover that the "loss," the "difference," or the "why" really *doesn't* matter. Not that much. Taking a long view of why some momentary frustration makes us angry may reveal that it is not worth all the adrenaline. On the other hand, if you really stand to lose a lot or the difference does matter, then you'll know that something so important requires a better, more positive response than uncontrollable anger. If it *really* matters, then it matters enough for you to meet the problem calmly and coolly and rationally.

Sharing your anger: Go to a third party if you are angry with another person. Get other viewpoints besides your own. One of anger's insidious tricks is to distort our view of reality just when we need to be in control of reality and ourselves. You'll assess your situation much better if you can see other sides to the problem, including other sides to your anger. It may take nerve to go to someone else and reveal your vulnerability, to tell someone that you feel like blowing your top or that you don't think you can control yourself. But the nerve it takes to do that is therapeutic in itself. It is a sign of strength. You are expressing your own power by seeking help from another person. And, once again, a sense of power will stymie the feeling of powerlessness that triggers anger.

Forgetting your anger: When you are angry at another person, the old motto "Forgive and forget" can actually work. Forgiving another is an act of power. By rising above the situation and telling the other party that you forgive, you show your own inner strength. You are saying, in effect, that you are stronger and bigger than the argument or dispute the two of you had. So forgive the other person and you'll find that it is easier to forget the incident.

*   *   *

Anger is not intrinsically destructive, even though it can play havoc with your emotions, distort your view of reality, and increase your stress level, which in turn is bad for your heart. In spite of all this, anger is a source of potential energy. After all, your heart is beating faster, just as if you were jogging or rowing a boat or making love. The excitement of being keyed up over something could be put to creative use, helping you to understand yourself or another human being, or life itself, more deeply than you did before. In fact, your "anger energy" just might bring you and the other person closer together. The key to it is to remember that anger, just like other feelings, can be expressed productively, communicated to another nonviolently, and used to enrich your life.

Type A Behavior

In the 1950s doctors Meyer Friedman and Ray Rosenman discovered that victims of cardiovascular disease exhibited certain behavior traits that people who did not have coronary heart disease lacked. Ever since their findings were published, this intriguing question about the link between behavior and heart disease has led researchers to conclude that there is some correlation between what Friedman and Rosenman called Type A behavior and heart attacks and strokes. Who are Type A people and what do they do? Basically, they are people who create stress for themselves by the way they go about their daily activities. Certain individuals seem to be prone to this stress-inducing life-style.

Friedman's caustic description of a Type A person is one who goes through life with a clenched fist holding a stopwatch. Someone who is constantly "off and running." A go-getter who can't slow down to enjoy things. An overly aggressive and competitive person who is always on the hunt for a challenge, always stalking an opponent to beat and triumph over. Even when Type A's play with their children, they're out to win. They usually overextend themselves with too many tasks, hobbies, commitments. Even making love is a performance, rather than an act of cooperation or submission.

Type A people never have enough time. No day is long enough, not for work, or play, or love. Type A's don't usually "sit down and think." Instead they think on the run. They usually have an unlimited number of things to get done. One of the distressing aspects of their tasks is that they are poorly defined jobs without clear-cut objectives. Furthermore, Type A's set unrealistic deadlines for themselves. They label their projects ASAP—as soon as possible. As you know, ASAPs usually lead to SNAFUs, and a SNAFU by any other name would smell of stress.

On the surface, though, Type A's smell of success. They conceal any worry, fear, or anxiety. Their exteriors are usually confident and resolute. They walk at a brisk clip; they radiate the aura of a winner. But underneath they would agree with poet Andrew Marvell, who said, "But at my back I always hear / Time's winged chariot hurrying near." Still, many Type A's delude themselves into thinking Time will not catch them. Unfortunately, their hearts can't take the pace, and it is their hearts that eventually catch up with them.

Heart attacks and strokes occur at a higher rate among Type A than Type B people, who exhibit the opposite set of characteristics in their behavior and attitudes toward life. Further studies of Type A and Type B people reveal that the Type A's have higher levels of cholesterol in their blood, higher blood pressure, smoke more cigarettes, and generally get less exercise than Type B's. In these areas, too, there is some yet-to-be-explained connection between this stress-creating behavior and other risk factors in heart disease.

You may be thinking, if you are Type A, "Well, what can be done? Aren't our personalities the real kernel of what we are, the individual that is truly us? Can they be changed without losing the unique person that I am?" The answer, which will not appeal to Type A's, is yes and no. The solution is not to chip away at your personality with a hammer and chisel, but to remodel your behavior. You *can* modify your behavior. You can learn new behavior patterns to replace the ones you have grown accustomed to. You can learn that just *being* is sometimes more important—and healthier—than *having*. You may even learn that some of the things you think are worth having really aren't. In fact, Friedman himself hoped that Type A's would eventually "see that it is more worthwhile to strive to obtain the things worth *being* rather than the things they believe are worth *having*; perhaps I could substitute love for their so easily aroused hostility; perhaps I could even cajole them into believing that equanimity is more to be desired than status enchancement.'' (Friedman's emphasis.)

Here are some techniques you might use to seduce or cajole yourself into more relaxed and easygoing behavior patterns.

1. **Loaf.** Make yourself do nothing at least once a week. Once a day is better. Walt Whitman boasted that he would ''loafe and invite my soul.'' Try it. Put yourself on ''idle.'' There is a Zen saying that you might put into practice. Don't just *do* something; *stand* there!

2. **Hide.** Find someplace where no one will see you, and then go there. Or find someplace where even if people do see you, they don't care. They don't know you. They let you alone. Discover some secret place and make it your retreat. Then get into the habit of going there regularly.

3. **Focus.** Concentrate your attention on the activity you are engaged in at the moment. Try to be as single-minded as you can. Worry about tomorrow tomorrow and five o'clock at five o'clock. The Japanese call it *mu*, which means ''nothingness'' or ''zero,'' and they achieve it while they make tea. In other words, when they make tea, they make tea. You can call it anything you want. But if you're making tea, make tea.

4. **Listen.** You could use a little *mu* when someone is talking to you. Focus on what that person is saying. And listen so that you actually *hear*. Don't plan what you will say next. Don't hurry the conversation along by whipping the speaker with your chain of ''uh-huh's.'' Don't interrupt. Just listen.

5. **Take it from the top.** Start over again. Make yourself restructure your days, especially if you haven't allowed enough time for everything. Cross some things out. Scale down your activities. Then, when you think you've gotten it more manageable, take it from the top again.

6. **Reminisce.** Go back over the day's events and think about them. Don't refight them. Just think about them. See how many you can recall. If they were pleasant, think about them a little longer.

7. **Smack your lips.** Eat slowly and taste your food. Savor it. Chew it sensuously. Consider how good it tastes. You're supposed to think about eating while you're eating.

8. **Read** *War and Peace*. Or *Moby Dick*. Or something else. The important point is that it be long. Type A's usually do not like to read long books.

9. Give up. Decide that it's okay to lose once in a while. Don't spend all your time with competitive people. Avoid them. Or if you can't, give in. Giving in works, too.

10. Get a cat. Mark Twain said that cats were created so that human beings would realize they aren't in control.

As you can see, some of these are simple and some are not, but then, changing your behavior is both simple and difficult. It is relatively easy to do something different. The hard part is to keep doing it. Getting into the habit of behaving like a Type B person is your goal. All of the above will make you take life easier, become less harried, help you to live more efficiently. Most of all, they should reduce your notion that time is so urgent. There are other activities besides these ten. You can think up your own if you don't like cats.

Time and Stress

Time waits for no one. We've all heard at our backs "Time's winged chariot hurrying near." Only in fantasies can we stop time or reverse time or speed it up. In reality we must cope with time as it really is, not as we would like it to be. Nevertheless, the way we use time can either cause us stress or be relaxing. *Time-use* is controllable, even though time itself is not. Many people stress themselves by not using time wisely and prudently. Since each of us uses time differently, it is not possible to map out a universal schedule on how to allocate time and expect it to be applicable to everyone's daily life.

A general principle, however, that does apply to all of us is that the degree of effective and efficient living put into a given unit of time will determine the amount of stress or relaxation that we experience. Stress comes from feeling harried, from a sense of time urgency, from feeling swamped with too much to do and not enough time to do it in. It isn't really necessary to slow yourself down so much as it is to manage your time more effectively so you can accomplish what's really important. A busy person is not necessarily under stress. Remember the old expression "Grace under pressure"? You can be under pressure but still in control of events and yourself. To get rid of stress does not mean to live slowly.

If we manage our time poorly, we will succumb to pressure,

lose our sense of accomplishment, and feel rushed or pushed. We may eventually feel so confused and indecisive that we think we are being overwhelmed by our jobs and responsibilities. We all know how apprehensive we can become when we think of the consequences that might arise from our having left some important matter undone. There is also a snowballing effect about all this. Worry, frustration, anxiety, irritability, and depression that come from our lack of accomplishment further inhibit our use of time effectively. No wonder we feel as if that chariot is going to run over us.

You have only twenty-four hours in every day. No one has any more. Here is a list of the general uses of time that ought to be incorporated, if possible, into every day.

1. Work.
2. Play: pleasure, something fun.
3. Exercise: physical activity that is good for you.
4. Leisure: doing nothing, idling.
5. Relaxation: resting, recharging your energy.
6. Sleep.
7. Eat.
8. Plan: scheduling these very activities. It may seem to you at first that planning is wasted time. But you will learn how untrue that is when you see how much time you save by spending it more efficiently.

A little exercise you might try is to draw a circle, then divide it like a clock into segments devoted to each of these eight activities. See what percentage of each day or twenty-four-hour period you spend in these activites.

It is really necessary for healthy, stress-free living that you make time for each of these activities in your average day. In fact, you must make time to make time. Have some period each day or week during which you plan ahead and see if you will be able to arrange all your commitments so that there is room for all eight of these time usages. This planning time is sacred and you should be alone, quiet, and undisturbed during it.

How do people waste time? There are an infinite number of ways! Remember: things that waste your time usually produce stress too. Time-wasters are stress-builders in disguise. Always consider things that waste your time as creating stress for yourself and think of yourself as reducing stress each time you plan and allocate the hours of your day.

Twenty-four-hour Clock

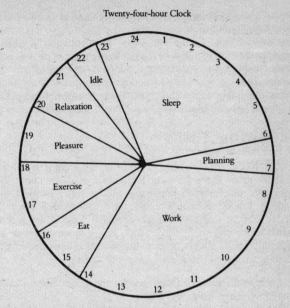

How to Use a Calendar

Even though we all learned how to read a calendar when we were children, especially so we could count the days until holidays and birthdays, very few of us ever learned how to *use* one. Calendars are meant to be used, not just read.

1. Don't schedule tasks back to back. Leave transition time between all events.
2. Record regularly occurring events several months or weeks in advance.
3. Inform people of time limits in advance. This way they know you are busy and won't take up extra minutes.
4. Do routine tasks at the same time every day. Group similar tasks together and you'll find they go a lot faster.
5. Block-in large chunks of time for high-priority tasks and tasks that are new to you that may take longer than you expected.

6. Intersperse dull jobs with exciting ones and fatiguing chores
    with easier ones.
7. Write in your leisure, pleasure, exercise, and relaxation
    activities as well as your tasks. Remember: You are plan-
    ning your entire time, not just the work segment of it.
8. Set priorities. Decide which tasks are absolutely necessary
    to do first and which can wait awhile. It's all right to put off
    till tomorrow things that can wait until tomorrow.

Delegating Tasks

One of the secrets to getting a lot of things accomplished is to
get others to do them for you. Business executives know this.
Supervisors and foremen practice it all the time. Even shrewd
parents will delegate chores around the house to each other and
their children so that they can get as much done in the shortest
possible time, and so that everybody has a sense of his or her
responsibilities. It always helps to know what is expected of you.

Here are ways to make delegating tasks easier.

1. Avoid omnipotence. Other people really can do projects as
    well as you if given the opportunity.
2. Resist perfectionism. Most things don't have to be perfect.
    An exception might be open-heart surgery!
3. Don't make yourself indispensable. It may boost your ego to
    think that a job can't be done without you, but if you lay
    your ego aside, you may realize that many jobs don't require
    your presence. Let others learn new tasks, too.
4. Explain most "whys" and only the absolutely necessary
    "hows." People need to know why, but they also need to
    exercise their own ingenuity in achieving the goal.
5. Give examples so that others know what you are talking
    about and what you expect. The clearer the instructions the
    better the chance the job will be done properly and to your
    personal satisfaction.
6. Don't oversupervise. "Supervise" already means to watch
    over. So don't overdo it. People work better if the boss isn't
    breathing down their necks.
7. Say no. Don't be afraid to assert your authority when neces-
    sary. If you give in to everyone's desires all the time, you
    may end up a doormat. Someone must be in charge, and the
    person in charge must know how to say no.

General Hints

As I said before, everyone uses and misuses time in unique ways. Time management is a very personal enterprise. But here are some general hints you should consider and put into practice wherever you can.

1. Take exercise breaks just as you would a coffee break. Take a short walk, do some stretching exercises. Better yet, plan an exercise period into each day. People who take breaks handle stress more efficiently and get more done.
2. Take time for comfortable, well-planned meals. Not only *what* you eat but *how* you eat is important for stressless living.
3. If you are ill, make time to get well. Visit your doctor, fill prescriptions, give yourself time to recuperate.
4. Time to rest is essential. Schedule regular short periods of relaxation. Plan to sleep. Instead of just ending up in bed each night, decide how much sleep you should get and plan a bedtime.
5. Allot transition time from one task or activity to another. You need time to catch your breath, even psychically, between projects.
6. A handy rule of thumb to reduce stress each day is leave about one-tenth of your daily schedule open. Call it "free time" or "flex time."
7. Somewhere in each day should be time just for yourself. You alone. Time when you owe nothing to anyone but yourself.
8. Do one task at a time until it is completed. Then go to the next task. But don't fall into the trap of trying to complete every task you undertake at one sitting.
9. It helps some people to keep only one task visible at a time. The mere sight of other jobs waiting to be done can cause panic and frustration. It also breaks your concentration and actually wastes time.
10. Approach your planning in terms of time rather than tasks. In other words, instead of saying "I have six things that I need to do," begin by saying "I have four hours. Now what can I reasonably do in those four hours?"

If you manage your time well, you will reduce stress. If you don't manage your time, you create stress for yourself. Put yourself in control of your time use, even though time itself is out of your hands. And by careful planning ahead, you will discover that you may actually have time *on* your hands.

Work Stress

Your level of stress at work may be due to any number of things. Karl Albrecht has distinguished eight factors that, if not properly balanced, can produce uncomfortable work situations that lead to stress. Each individual has a comfort zone beyond which there is too much or too little of a given factor. If you go beyond your comfort zone, you will experience stress. Analyze each of the eight to see how they balance one another in your own life situation. You may discover that one or more need to be modified to reduce stress. If in some cases a factor at work is nonmodifiable, you may need to compensate for it at home. For example, if your job requires you to work in solitude, you will not be able to increase "human contact" at work, but you might build into your social life or homelife ways to be with more people. The important point is to avoid "overloading" any one factor to the point where it causes stress.

1. **Work load.** Too many tasks for the time allotted or too few tasks for the time allotted. Not having enough to do can be boring, makes the time pass slowly, and can cause stress.
2. **Physical.** Are you comfortable at work? Or is the environment too noisy, too hot, too cold, polluted? Must you stand all day or sit on an uncomfortable chair?
3. **Job status.** A celebrity who is too well known and too much in demand may have as much stress, because of high status, as a garbage collector who wants more recognition.
4. **Accountability.** This means the amount of risk there is in your job versus the amount of control you have over those risks. Some jobs like air-traffic controllers are high in accountability; others, like envelope stuffers, entail very little risk.
5. **Task variety.** In some jobs you never know what will occur next and there is a wide variety of things that keep you busy. These kinds of jobs may need more structure to reduce

stress. Other jobs are so dull and routine that there is very little feeling of accomplishment. In this case, you may have to add more variety either at work or at home.

6. **Human contact.** Different people need different amounts of human contact. Lighthouse keepers don't have much contact, but then maybe the type of person who does this work doesn't require much. Schoolteachers have a lot. If you are in a job that has the wrong amount for you, you will have to supplement it with compensating activities during your nonwork hours.

7. **Physical challenge.** Police, for example, have a lot; librarians very little. The balance in your total life between physical and nonphysical is what is important. If you do not have this balance, an exercise program every day may be the key.

8. **Mental challenge.** All human beings need to be mentally challenged. If you don't get it at work, you should have some hobby or pastime that provides it for you.

Many of my patients who are recovering from heart attacks or heart surgery frequently ask during their visits to the Institute about their ability to return to work. They have two major concerns. First, will their physical capacity enable them to do their former job or will there be significant physical limitations? Second, and usually of even more concern, is there a possible connection between their work and their heart condition that brought them to us in the first place? Our goal in the cardiac-conditioning program of the Institute is to return people to as normal a life as possible—work and play alike. When there is concern that the type of employment might have been responsible for their heart problems, the goal often becomes difficult to attain. Like everything we have said in this chapter on the Stress Factor, a lot depends on how the person perceives his or her work. If the job is perceived as enjoyable, rewarding, and worthwhile, it is probable that the occupation is low in the risk category for producing the heart condition. If, on the other hand, all the negative factors discussed above are present in the job, the likelihood of job-related stress contributing to the cardiac condition is great. Complete recovery and rehabilitation can occur only through drastic modification of the job situation.

8 The Weight Factor

Stop! If you were just now planning to thumb on to the next chapter, hold it! No one likes to admit he or she is overweight. But what was your score on the Heart Test for question 10? Go back and look. If it was 4 or 2, *you* are overweight, and could profit from this chapter. If your score was 0, you are not *now* overweight, but you ought to read on and pick up the handy tips and pointers for *keeping* your weight at its ideal level.

Fat people are not jolly. Even though the stereotype persists that they are, fat people we have treated at the Arizona Heart Institute attest to the sad fact that American society is not cut out for them. The media put such importance on being thin—usually expressed as "young"—and modern architecture, chairs, airplanes, telephone booths, restaurant booths, and so forth, are designed for the lean and trim. Seldom have fashions catered to the heavyset. And as Americans become more sports- and exercise-minded, the overweight are frequently left behind on Saturday outings, vacation plans, and many social gatherings.

The proliferation of weight-reduction plans that have swept the country in recent years also attests to the fact that more and more obese people want to lose weight. Unfortunately, great amounts of time and money are invested in weight-loss programs with meager results. Ninety-eight percent of those who successfully lose more than thirty pounds regain most of that weight within two years. Twelve billion dollars is spent annually on food gimmicks that don't work. And because so many people have been duped by programs or dupe themselves by thinking that initial weight loss is all that is required, 40 percent of the American population is still overweight to the point that it interferes with their health. Obesity is correlated with many health problems in the United States.

Dangers

In addition to the bona fide diet plans that are available, there are an appalling number of fad diets, near starvation diets, and chic diet clubs that do considerable harm. Here are some of the problems that might occur if you get lured into the wrong program without the proper supervision. Remember that something as important as the food you eat should be regulated only with expert advice from someone qualified to give it.

1. **Medical problems** may arise if you are not under a physician's supervision while losing significant amounts of weight. You should not lose more than two to four pounds per week. You can seriously harm your health over a long period of time if your meals are not nutritionally balanced.
2. **New behaviors and values** must be learned along with the methods of losing weight if you are to embark on a life-style that will keep those pounds from returning.
3. **Standardized programs** that do not tailor the diet to the individual's own health needs can be dangerous.
4. **A support system** is crucial to facilitate and maintain weight loss. Solo programs can be defeating and demoralizing.

The Arizona Heart Institute diet for weight management was designed to avoid these problems and at the same time allow you to lose weight and discover ways to maintain your new weight by modifying your life-style and eating habits. Our weight-management program is a multidisciplinary system that in addition to dieting, includes exercising, behavior modification, and education. You will learn how to "take charge" of your eating behavior, acquire self-confidence, increase your self-awareness, become more in control. If you follow our instructions you will acquire new attitudes and concepts about food, learning to view it as sustenance for the body, not a substitute for emotional gratification. We will give you tips on shopping for food, cooking, eating out, aerobic exercises, and ways to create for yourself an active life that will ensure weight stabilization.

In other words, your Heart Test score need not remain as high as it is now. Diet, exercise, and psychological conditioning can bring your weight into acceptable ranges and at the same time reduce your cholesterol, triglycerides, blood pressure, and sugar levels.

But before you actually begin cooking your new meals and stretching your "new" muscles, you must be psychologically conditioned for a total weight-management life-style. There is much more involved than just the number of cinnamon muffins you eat per week and the number of times you jog around a cinder track. The next sections of this chapter should be read carefully to gain greater self-awareness about your habits, values, environment, friends, and family. These, too, are significant components in your weight and fitness program. No one is fit or becomes fit in a vacuum. We live in real houses, engage in real hobbies and habits, spend time with real people, have specific memories and images of ourselves that act either positively or negatively toward our goal of fitness and ideal weight.

Your Diet-Weight History

There are no fat genes. If you are overweight today, you cannot blame it on inheritance. Mother and Dad did not make you fat genetically. However, there are fat foods. Perhaps your history of being overweight began with the meals your parents served you as a child. Your current eating habits and body build have a past. By filling out the Diet-Weight History Inventory below, you will expand your consciousness regarding your overweight problem. There are many personal aspects of diet and weight you need to be aware of before you begin your program. There is no score to this exercise. It is solely for your own information.

DIET-WEIGHT HISTORY INVENTORY

1. Current height _____ and weight _____
2. Weight one year ago _____
3. Weight at age 21 _____
4. What is the most you have ever weighed? _____When? _____
5. What is the least you have weighed since age 21? _____
   When? _____Why? _____
6. Have you lost or gained weight recently? _____ How many
   pounds? _____
   Why? _____
7. What do you think a reasonable weight would be? _____
8. What do others say is a reasonable weight? _____
9. How long have you been overweight? _____
10. Were you overweight as a child? _____
11. When have you weighed what you wanted? _____
12. Do you consider your body frame to be small, medium, large?
13. Do you think that you are overweight right now?
    If yes, do you eat because of
       a. hunger
       b. habit
       c. boredom
       d. nervousness
       e. stress
       f. giving up smoking
       g. other
14. What foods are you allergic to? _____
15. What foods do you dislike? _____
16. What foods are your overindulgences? _____
17. Do you wear dentures? _____ If not, how many teeth are you
    missing? _____
18. What foods do you have problems chewing or what foods do you
    avoid because you are unable to chew them? _____
19. Do you have digestive problems caused from any food? _____
    If yes, what? _____
20. Which foods cause it? _____
21. What foods do you not eat because of your religious beliefs? ____
    _____
22. Are you a vegetarian? _____
23. Are you a diabetic? _____
24. Do you have an ulcer? _____
25. Who does the grocery shopping for you? _____

26. Who prepares your food? _____
27. How often do you eat meals away from home? _____What meals? _____
28. Are your meals usually eaten
    alone _____
    with a family member
       spouse _____ children _____ other _____
    with a friend _____
    with business associates _____
29. Are you a fast or slow eater? _____
30. Do you take second helpings? _____
31. Do you serve family-style? _____
32. Are you currently following a special diet? _____ If yes, what kind? _____
33. From whom did you get the information about this diet? _____
34. What types of special diets have you followed in the past? _____
    _____
35. If you were ever on a diet for weight reduction were you successful in losing weight? _____ If not, why not? _____
36. Were your parents overweight? _____Why? _____
37. Is your spouse overweight? _____Why? _____
38. Are your children overweight? _____Why? _____
39. Do you believe that your job contributes in any way to your weight problem? _____ How? _____
40. Do you currently exercise? _____What kind? _____ How often? _____

Memories

   Food does not go just to your stomach. It goes to your mind as well, where it is locked in your memory and motivates you in your eating habits. Think back to when you were ten; what were your favorite foods? What made you gag? What were your family's favorite meals, the ones everyone "ooohed and aaahed" over when they were served? What did your mother serve you when you were sick? You may not consciously think about these, but subconscious memories of them continue to influence your eating style. Other memories come from advertisements for certain foods you've seen on TV, in magazines, and on the packages themselves. Remember Elsie the cow? She made you want to drink milk. Remember the foods that would give you "mythical muscles"? Spinach was supposed to make you as strong as Popeye, even though not many of us ever asked *why* we needed to be as strong as Popeye. Some foods were the foods "of champions." Others promised to build strong bodies twelve ways. Later they added some more ways. Certain food gave you curly hair. Certain food was good for your eyesight. Or so they said.

Eating, cooking, and choosing food are complex acts partially shaped by your past. Luckily, you are not chained to your past. Much can be modified. When you are trying to make a food change, and a strong feeling results, think back about past influences and habits that you may associate with that food. Then work on your thoughts, habits, and associations that surround that particular food or eating custom.

Here are some of the more common types of memories that influence our eating style:

1. Childhood associations
2. Pleasing our parents
3. Food we were served when we were sick
4. Treat food; reward snacks
5. Ethnic or regional foods
6. Mythical muscle food in the media

How to Change Your Eating Style

Your present eating style may be one that encourages you to overeat. Learn to identify the cues that trigger overeating, then do something about them. Here are some remedies you can use to stifle them. Choose the ones that apply best to your overeating problems and work on one a week until you have eliminated them from your eating style.

Where you eat. Eat only while sitting down at a proper eating place and with the proper eating utensils. This will limit your eating to one place in the house and thereby cut down on the times you are tempted to eat in other rooms. This technique also applies to tasting food while you cook. Don't. You should not eat at the stove.

How to eat alone. People who eat alone tend to overeat for a number of reasons: to pass the time, to use food as a substitute for companionship, to forget possible loneliness. If you eat alone, don't do anything else but eat. Don't read, listen to the radio, watch TV, or talk on the phone. These distractions will keep you from supervising how much you are eating.

Conscious eating. Practice conscious eating. Eat slowly, chew slowly, set the fork or spoon down between bites. Savor your food. Acknowledge the activity of eating.

Schedule your meals. Write down in advance the meals and snacks planned for the following day. Be sure to eat at least three meals each day. Before each meal or snack, review the plan and mentally okay the foods you've selected to eat.

Ambush those binges. You can eliminate binge eating by hesitating between the desire to eat and the act of eating. When you get the desire to eat, immediately engage in a diverting activity.

Eat small. You know you'll lose weight if you eat "small," but how to do it? Serve small portions of food on a small plate. Use a seven-inch plate instead of a nine-inch one. Serve your helpings from the stove rather than family-style. Seeing all that food on the table encourages you to want seconds. Leave some food on your plate. No matter what your mother said about that, no matter how sorry you feel or whoever is starving anywhere, it is okay to leave some food on your plate. Lastly, leave the table when you have finished eating. If you sit around to chat, you'll probably end up nibbling on the leftovers.

Unpair your stimuli. Some of your eating is associated with other activities or places. Like Pavlov's dogs that learned to salivate when bells rang and lights flashed, you, too, have bells and lights. For example, many people always snack on something when they watch TV. For them the TV is stimulus to eating. Some people always have to grab a late-night snack after the theater. Others always munch on something during their coffee breaks at work. Whatever you have paired with your need to eat, become aware of it, and start controlling yourself in those situations. Make up your mind that the next time the situation occurs, you WILL NOT EAT.

Resisting Grocery Store Temptations

Whatever type of heart diet you are on, you're still going to have to go shopping for food, and as you probably know already, the grocery store can tempt you off your diet as easily as your refrigerator. In fact, grocery stores and refrigerators are in cahoots. Be wary of both. Here are some hints for avoiding grocery store temptations.

1. Go shopping with a list. Don't ad-lib! Chances of buying items that are not allowed on your diet are greater if you go shopping on the spur of the moment.
2. Shop once weekly. Stock up for seven days so you won't have to go back. The less time you spend in a grocery store the better.
3. Shop when you're not hungry. Hunger pangs gnawing at your stomach can delude you into thinking you need to buy more food than is absolutely necessary.
4. Shop with a friend. Go with someone who knows you are on a diet and with whom you can discuss tempting purchases.
5. If you are tempted, ask yourself, "Is this food really necessary?" Make yourself come up with some pretty good reasons for buying an item not on your approved shopping list.

Altering Your Environment

Your living environment can make or break your diet. So often we are oblivious to the physical space in which we live, cook, and eat. Here are some tips for redesigning your home for maximum diet success.

1. **Plan one place** in the house where you will diet. Do all your eating there. This will get you out of the habit of snacking and nibbling all over the house—the bedroom, the living room, the TV room.
2. **Store your food** to minimize temptations. Put the highest calorie and/or most tempting foods in hard-to-reach places. Use opaque jars and bags for storage. Keep foods that are okay for your diet in front in clear containers.
3. **Eliminate as many temptations as possible.** For example, move the TV out of the kitchen. Put candy dishes away. Don't leave crackers or cookies in plain view. Buy kitchen containers with rural scenes rather than seasonal feasts on them. It's less tempting to look at a haystack than a pumpkin pie.

4. **Have alternative activities handy** for those moments around the house when you have nothing to do and are tempted to nibble—crafts, chores, books, taking walks. It doesn't matter what you do, just do something to take your mind off eating.

The Knack of Snacking

It's okay to snack. In fact, we recommend it so that if you really get hungry, you won't be tempted to gorge yourself at the next meal. It's better to be a nibbler than a gorger. Here are some safety rules, however, so that you don't snack yourself off your diet.

1. Do not *buy* snack foods. Make low-calorie fun foods from scratch in small quantities.
2. Consult our Low-Calorie Snacks list in the diet section of this chapter.
3. "Bank" your calories. If you know a special occasion is coming up, such as an all-day picnic or an evening cocktail party, where there will be snack food, get ready for it in advance. Begin seven to ten days ahead of time and reduce the number of calories you consume each day so that when the big occasion arrives, you can splurge. It's like saving up calories so that you can "spend," that is, eat, them later on. For example, if you regularly eat cheese on your luncheon sandwich, leave one slice off each day for ten days. One slice of cheese equals 100 calories. At the end of the ten-day period, you will have banked 1,000 calories. You can add to your banking of calories by exercising more during this period, also. A cardinal rule here is that no "deficit spending" is allowed. Follow President Reagan's fiscal policy in this and don't let yourself eat beyond your diet—that is, more than you are allowed—and then try to make up for it later by reducing your calories. "Later" doesn't work!
4. Evening snacks: Plan a schedule of activities for your evenings in order to give yourself less time for eating.
5. Midnight snackers: Plan your low-calorie snack before you go to bed, so if you get up during the night you won't fumble around groggily in the dark, and "accidentally" grab the chocolate cake. Avoid liquids in the evening so

your chances of making it through the night without waking up are better. If you do wake up, wait a few minutes before getting up. When you do eat that snack, eat it at your regular eating place.

How to Eat Out and Not Go Off Your Diet

You don't need to eat every meal at home just because you are on a diet. Restaurants, like grocery stores, are filled with temptations, but you can learn to overcome them and stay on your diet. Sometime when you are not hungry, go to a coffee shop or small diner. Order a cup of coffee or a diet soda. Sit where you can observe the entire place and notice how the restaurant encourages eating. Notice the displays of cakes and pies, the flashy ads over the counter, the sugary soft drinks bubbling through their tanks, the waiters and waitresses who suggest extra foods, especially desserts. When eating out you must be aware of how restaurants encourage you to overeat.

Here are some hints for eating out and successfully ordering low-calorie foods.

1. Go to restaurants you know serve meals that can be tailored to your diet. Avoid the specialty restaurants that cater to high-caloric tastes.
2. If you frequent the same restaurants, you can get to know their menus. Then you can plan your meal ahead. Just tell the waiter or waitress what you want without looking at the menu. If you must look at a menu, learn to look only at the entrees and salads.
3. Ask for foods that are okay for your diet even if they aren't on the menu, such as grilled chicken, margarine, or a cheese, lettuce, and tomato sandwich at Burger King.
4. Order first before you hear the mouthwatering meals your friends will order.
5. Move breads to the far side of the table or ask the waitress to remove them.
6. If a plate comes with a food item that you cannot eat, have the waiter take it back.
7. Be assertive and ask for what you want. Remember you have a right to be thin. Do not apologize or become aggres-

sive. Make simple statements beginning with "I" that let others know how you feel.

8. Practice ahead of time what you will answer to the following food-encouraging statements:

What would you like for dessert?
Put some vodka in that soda. I don't want to drink alone.
Try some of this cake. It's great!
Let's go to Captain Bill's smorgasbord for dinner.
Oh, go ahead and enjoy yourself. You can always diet tomorrow.

Support While Losing Weight

Whenever you are on a diet, it is crucial that you get support for your positive actions and accomplishments. You have two sources of support: other people and yourself. First, let's consider how other people can help or hinder you in getting the support and encouragement you need for successful dieting.

1. Some people will encourage you to eat for *their* needs or because they do not know better. For example, some people use food, as you used to, for emotional gratification. If they invite you along for ice cream, you will either have to refuse or say you'll go along but will not have any.
2. Some people may nag you about your slipups. Be aware of who they are and either avoid them as much as possible, or don't let them know about your slipups, or . . .
3. State your position to them simply and clearly. Use assertiveness techniques so they understand how you feel about their remarks. Here are several assertiveness guidelines that should work for you.

   a. Freely reveal your feelings to the other—such as "I am happy that . . ." or "I am sad that . . ."
   b. Use language that is open, honest, and direct. Make it appropriate to the person you are talking with. Begin your sentences with "I."
   c. Do not be aggressive, smart-alecky, or violent.
   d. Make things happen to you as a result of your remarks, rather than let things be done to you.

For example, you could say, "It is important to me to follow my diet, no thank you." "I don't care for any, thanks." "The diet is really hard for me. Please comment on my progress not my failures."

4. Ask directly for "strokes." Ask your spouse to hold your hand or hug you.

5. Ask indirectly for support. For example, ask someone to go for a walk with you as an alternative to nibbling. Invite someone over to spend the evening with you watching TV if you think you'll be snacking out of loneliness.

6. Teach others how to support you. This may be new behavior for them. Here are some ways to teach them how.

   a. Ask for what you want. Be assertive. Tell them you need a hug or a compliment.

   b. Thank them for every little bit of support they show you.

   c. Pay attention to the underlying messages in another's behavior. For example, if someone wants to buy you a beer out of appreciation, tell them you accept the appreciation but will have to refuse the beer. Suggest a nonfood option.

7. Learn how to accept compliments rather than negate them. If you show your awkwardness or embarrassment at being complimented, other people will soon learn not to compliment you. And compliments are what you need. Here are some samples of how to field compliments successfully.

   a. You certainly have tried hard.
      Reply: Thanks, I feel good about my efforts.

   b. That was a wonderful salad.
      Reply: I really enjoy making salads. Thanks.

   c. You're sure looking good these days.
      Reply: Yes, my diet is really working.

Self-Support

Supporting yourself is just as necessary as getting support from others. Many of the ways we support ourselves are similar to the ways we build a positive self-image. The reason you need self-support right now is that you may have been using food as emotional nourishment. Now that you have learned to relegate food to bodily nourishment, you will need to replace it with the right kind of psychic nourishment. A healthy self-image, positive, forward-looking, confident, and self-assured, is vital to your diet program.

1. Engage in things that are enjoyable. Some of these will replace the eating binges that you formerly used for enjoyment. Also, we feel better about ourselves when we are having fun. Play is not just for children.

2. Keep your mind active and alert. Read, take classes, learn a skill, acquire new knowledge. Boredom and lethargy are open invitations to poor eating behavior. The food you need is mental, not physical.

3. In a given week, make a note or a chart of your accomplishments, not your failures. There will be failures now and then, but forget them. Remind yourself of your successes.

4. Solve your problems. Look for solutions. Start to improve your life wherever necessary. Bemoaning problems or feeling sorry for yourself leads to feelings of inadequacy and temptations to drown your misery in lasagna.

5. Associate with people who are fun and give you a sense of self-esteem. Avoid deadbeats, sad sacks, and killjoys. You need the example and role-model behavior of people who enjoy themselves and have a positive self-image themselves.

6. Act as though the positive self-image is already present. Look at people when talking to them and sit or stand in a confident posture.

7. Pay attention to your physical appearance. Dress as a thin person with a positive image. Overweight people frequently dress in a style that shouts, "I'm fat! Why should I bother to try to look nice?" A defeatist attitude expressed in your clothing is never in style.

8. Take an interest in other people. Do things for them and pay *them* compliments. Too much self-absorption is dangerous. We can all find reasons to be miserable with ourselves. So the more time you spend with and for others, the less time you've got for self-pity and that self-defeating, woe-is-me attitude.

9. Study other people, especially their backgrounds and how they got to wherever they are—both the successes and the failures. Then compare your own story with theirs in terms

of learning what is really important to you in life. Decide what you need to do to get where you want to be.

10. Write goals and objectives in addition to your weight management ones. Chart out courses of action that will get you there. Don't dwell on the negative, or past failures. No one is perfect. Take command of your life and move it ahead.

Most of all, persevere in thinking and acting as a confident, physically fit, positive-minded individual. It isn't easy to change a negative self-image into a new one. Don't expect transformations overnight. But start now. You won't learn how to *think* and *act* like a thin, fit person just by losing a few pounds. Losing weight will only make you *look* fit. Being and staying fit *as a total person* must register in your mind, not just on the bathroom scale.

Weight-Management Diet

Heredity, life-style, eating habits, and your own metabolism all play some part in determining whether or not you have the proper weight for your age, sex, and height. Food alone is not the culprit, but a sensible diet, structured to reduce calories, is an essential component for any weight-management program. As you have seen already, successful dieters do more than just plan low-calorie meals. They have an outlook, an attitude about themselves that reshapes their entire life and encourages them to live in ways that take the unwanted pounds off and keep them off. Their diet is a diet for life, not just for a week or a month.

The weight-management diet in this section is meant to be a diet for life. It is a low-calorie diet that does not sacrifice the pleasure of eating for the reward of being thin. It allows you to enjoy meals *and* limit your caloric intake. If you combine this diet with an exercise program to burn up calories, you will become a champion at regulating the number of calories you consume with the number you burn. You'll know which foods are higher in calories than others, you'll know how to "bank" your calories for special occasions when you know you will want to eat more than is normally allowed, and you'll have an exercise routine that periodically and faithfully uses up calories so you maintain your desired weight.

People frequently ask what a calorie really is. A calorie is a unit of measure. One calorie is the amount of heat needed to raise the temperature of one gram of water by one degree centigrade. The energy you store in your body and use up in physical activity is measured in calories. It takes a deficit of 3,500 calories to lose one pound of fat. You can lose the pound either by eating 3,500 calories less, or by burning up 3,500 calories through exercise.

Here are some general instructions you should follow when planning your meals.

1. Obtain all the necessary nutrients by eating a wide variety of foods from the four basic food groups. Each day you should have two servings from the low-fat milk and dairy group, two from the high-protein group, three to four from the whole grain bread and cereal groups, and four from the fresh fruit and vegetable group (one, a dark green or deep yellow vegetable for vitamin A; another, a citrus fruit, tomato, cantaloupe, strawberries, or broccoli for vitamin C).

2. Emphasize whole grain bread and cereal products in your daily meals; for example, 100 percent whole wheat bread, brown rice.

3. Simple sugars, candy, syrup, jellies, honey, and most desserts are quite high in calories and are poor sources of vitamins, minerals, and fiber. In order for you to obtain all the necessary nutrients while you are reducing your calorie intake, these foods must be restricted.

4. Read labels carefully! The ingredients listed on a manufacturer's label begin with the ingredient found in the largest quantity within the product and proceed in descending order to that ingredient that is in the smallest quantity. Check the section in this book How to Read Labels, starting on page 169.

5. Eat only those foods that are permitted in your diet.

6. Eat only the amounts specified. A small, inexpensive food or postal scale will help you with portion sizes, especially meat.

7. Use standard measuring cups and spoons to measure your food. Measure the amount you eat *after* the food is cooked, and without any liquid.

8. Buy the leanest cuts of meat. All meat, poultry, and fish should be either baked, broiled, or boiled—not fried. A roasting rack is essential for most cooking. All visible fat and skin should be removed before eating.

9. Eat only those gravies and sauces that are made with allowed ingredients, and then eat them sparingly.

Food Exchange Lists

The diet foods listed below have been adjusted to also reduce your cholesterol and saturated fat consumption. These foods can be used to make up a well-balanced diet. Follow these lists carefully, avoiding any foods that are not listed here.

LOW CHOLESTEROL, LOW SATURATED FAT—AMERICAN DIABETIC ASSOCIATION FOOD EXCHANGE LISTS

LIST 1: MILK EXCHANGES:

Skim milk: Calories = 80

Skim milk	1 cup
Skim milk, evaporated	1/2 cup
Skim milk, powdered	1/4 cup
Skim milk, buttermilk	1 cup

(Prepared with allowed fats and skim milk)

LIST 2: VEGETABLE EXCHANGES:

"A" vegetables: Insignificant carbohydrate or calories. Eat raw as desired. Limit to 3 cups cooked.

Asparagus	Escarole
Bamboo sprouts	*Kale
Bean sprouts	Lettuce
Beet greens	Mushrooms
*Broccoli	*Mustard greens
Brussels sprouts	Okra
*Cabbage	Pepper, green, red, or chili
Cauliflower	Radishes
Celery	Sauerkraut
*Chard	Scallions
Chayote	*Spinach

*Contains carotene for vitamin A.

*Chicory	String beans
*Collard greens	Summer squash
Cucumbers	*Tomatoes
*Dandelion greens	Turnip greens
Eggplant	*Watercress
Endive	Wax beans

"B" vegetables: Calories = 36. One serving = 1/2 cup.

Artichoke (medium)	Pumpkin
Beets	Rutabagas
Carrots	Turnips
Mixed vegetables	Water chestnuts
Onions	Winter squash
Peas	

LIST 3: FRUIT EXCHANGES:

Calories = 40.

Berries

Blackberries	1/2 cup	Loganberries	1/2 cup
Blueberries	1/2 cup	Raspberries	1/2 cup
Gooseberries	2/3 cup	Strawberries	2/3 cup or 10 large

Citrus

Grapefruit	1/2 small or 1/2 cup	Mandarin (water or juice pack)	3/4 cup
Lemon	1 large		
Lime	1 large or 2 small	Orange	1 small or 1/2 cup
		Tangerine	1 large or 2 small

Dried

*Apricots	4 halves		
Dates	2	Pears	2 halves
Figs	1 small	Prunes	2 medium
Peaches	2 halves	Raisins	2 tablespoons

---

*Contains carotene for vitamin A.

Juice (unsweetened)

Apple or cider	1/3 cup
Cranberry (low-calorie)	1/4 cup
Grape	1/4 cup
Grapefruit	1/2 cup
Lemon, fresh	1/2 cup
Orange	1/2 cup
Pineapple	1/3 cup
Prune	1/4 cup

Melons

*Cantaloupe, 6-inch diameter	1/4
Casaba, 6-inch diameter	1/4
Honeydew, 7-inch diameter	1/8
Watermelon	1 slice (5 inches by 3/4 inch)

Other

Apple, 2-inch diameter	1
Applesauce (unsweetened)	1/2 cup
*Apricots	2 medium
Banana	1/2 small
Cherries	10 large
Cherries, sour red	1/2 cup
Figs	1 medium
Fruit cocktail, water- or juice-packed	1/2 cup
Grapes	12
Guava	1 medium
*Mango	1 small
*Nectarine	1 large
*Papaya	1/3 medium
*Papaya pulp	1/2 cup
*Peach	2 halves
*Peach, sliced	1/2 cup
Pear	2 halves
Pineapple, fresh or juice-packed	1/2 cup
Pineapple, sliced	1 thick slice
Plums	2 whole
*Pomegranate	1 medium
Prunes	2 medium

*Contains carotene for vitamin A.

LIST 4: BREAD EXCHANGES:

Calories = 68.

Bagel	1/2
†Biscuit, 2-inch roll	1
Bread	1 slice
Cereal, cooked	1/2 cup
Cereal, dry flakes, puffed	3/4 cup
†Corn bread, 1-1/2-inch cube	1
Crackers, graham	2
Crackers, oyster (1/2 cup)	20
Crackers, round (1-1/2-inch)	6
Crackers, saltine (2-inch square)	5
Crackers, soda (2-1/2-inch square)	3
English muffin	1/2
Flour	2-1/2 tablespoons
†Muffin, 2-inch diameter	1
Rice or grits, cooked	1/2 cup
Spaghetti, noodles, etc.	1/2 cup
†Tortilla, corn or wheat (6-inch)	1 small

---

†Prepared with allowed fats and skim milk.

Starchy Vegetables
Baked beans, no pork	1/4 cup
Beans, lima, navy, etc. (dried, cooked)	1/2 cup
Corn	1/3 cup
Parsnips	2/3 cups
Peas, split, etc. (dried, cooked)	1/2 cup
Popcorn	1 cup
*Potatoes, sweet or yams	1/2 cup
Potatoes, white	1 small
Potatoes, white, mashed	1/2 cup

Desserts
Angel food cake	1 ounce
Sherbet	1/3 cup
Tapioca (dry)	2 tablespoons

---

*Contains carotene for vitamin A.

LIST 5: MEAT EXCHANGES:

Calories = approximately 70 per serving.

Cottage cheese, low-fat	1/2 cup
Cheese, part-skim (limit 6 ounces per week)	1 ounce
Egg (limit yolk to 3 per week)	1
Egg substitute, low-cholesterol	1/4 cup
Fish—haddock, halibut, etc.	1 oz.
Salmon, water-packed tuna	1/2 cup
Meat—lean and well trimmed	
Beef, ham, lamb, pork	1 ounce } *Limit to 3 ounces five times per week.*
Peanut butter (old-fashioned style) (limit 1 tablespoon daily)	1 tablespoon
Poultry without skin	
Chicken, turkey, Cornish hen, squab	1 oz.
Shellfish (substitute for red meat)	
Crab, lobster	1/4 cup } *Shrimp is allowed once per week.*
Oysters, clams, shrimp	5 small
Turkey-based products	
Hot dog	1
Cold cuts (check the labels)	2 slices
Veal	1 oz.

LIST 6: FAT EXCHANGES:

Calories = 45.

Margarine (made with liquid corn oil, cottonseed, soybean, or safflower oil)	1 teaspoon
Mayonnaise	1 teaspoon
Nuts (walnuts, almonds, peanuts, pecans)	6 small
Oils (corn, cottonseed, soybean, safflower, sunflower, sesame)	1 teaspoon
Salad dressings made with allowed oils	1 tablespoon
Sesame seeds	1 tablespoon
Sunflower seeds	1-1/2 tablespoons
Tartar sauce	1 tablespoon

FREE FOODS: EAT AS DESIRED

Bouillon or clear broth

Coffee or tea (if not decaffeinated, limit to 3 cups daily)

Condiments

Cranberries, unsweetened

Extracts

Gelatin, unsweetened

Herbs

Lemon

Mustard

Pepper

Pickles, unsweetened

Rhubarb, unsweetened

Saccharin

Seasonings

Soft drinks, sugar-free

Spices

Sucaryl

Vinegar

Three Low-Calorie Diet Plans

Here are three low-calorie diet plans, one for 1,000 calories, one for 1,200, and one for 1,400. After each basic diet, we have outlined a sample meal plan for an entire week of nutritionally good eating.

1,000-CALORIE DIET PLAN

BREAKFAST

4 ounces orange juice (or 1 serving of a citrus fruit or juice from list)

*1 slice whole wheat toast (or other bread exchange)

Choose one of the following: 1 egg (limit 3 per week), ¼ cup Egg Beaters, 1 ounce part-skim milk cheese (limit 6 ounces per week), ½ cup *low-fat* cottage cheese, ⅓ cup (2 ounces) fish (if canned, must be water-packed), 1 tablespoon old-fashioned peanut butter (limit to 1 tablespoon daily)

LUNCH

Choose one of the following: 2 ounces fish or chicken (no skin), 1 ounce turkey-based cold cuts (e.g., turkey ham), 1 ounce (slice) part-skim milk cheese, ½ cup low-fat cottage cheese, 1 cup skim milk yogurt, 1 tablespoon old-fashioned peanut butter

1 slice whole grain bread (or other bread exchange)

"A" vegetable (as desired)

1 apple or fruit exchange

DINNER

3 ounces fish, poultry (no skin), or veal; five times per week you may have 3 ounces of lean, well-trimmed beef, pork, ham, Canadian bacon, lamb, venison, rabbit, or shellfish (shrimp is limited to 3 ounces per week)

1 small baked potato (or other bread exchange)

"A" vegetable (as desired)

---

*Note: If you have just cereal and skim milk for breakfast, count the cereal as a bread exchange and have an additional ounce of meat at lunch or dinner.

½ cup "B" vegetable from exchange list
1 fruit exchange

Recommended daily: 2 cups skim milk or 2 skim milk exchanges.
Permitted daily: 1 fat exchange and 1 teaspoon low-sugar jam or jelly.

Sample Meal Plan—1,000 Calories

Day	Breakfast	Lunch	Dinner
1	½ banana ¾ cup corn flakes 1 cup skim milk Coffee or tea	Open-faced turkey ham and cheese sandwich (1 slice each wheat toast, turkey ham, Jarlsberg cheese; sprouts, lettuce, tomato, mustard; 1 teaspoon mayonnaise if desired) 1 apple 1 cup skim milk	4 ounces broiled halibut with lemon ½ cup carrots ½ cup herbed rice Tossed salad/low-calorie dressing ½ cup juice-packed pears
2	4 ounces orange juice 1 slice wheat toast 1 tablespoon legal* peanut butter 1 cup skim milk	Assorted relishes (celery, cucumber, carrot sticks) ½ cup low-fat cottage cheese ½ cup juice-packed pineapple 5 RyKrisps 1 cup skim milk	3 ounces pork chop/½ cup sage dressing ½ cup green peas Spinach salad ½ cup unsweetened applesauce
3	½ grapefruit 1 serving Oro wheat apple-cinnamon oatmeal	Cheese crisp (12-inch tortilla, 2 ounces part-skim cheese; tomatoes, green onions, chilies, lettuce, and 1 tablespoon guacamole, yogurt	4 ounces roast chicken (no skin) Broccoli Baked potato 1 teaspoon margarine Fresh fruit

*Made with ingredients allowed on your individual diet.

	1 cup skim milk Coffee or tea	dip, or diet dressing) 1 peach 1 cup skim milk	
4	Cantaloupe wedge ¼ cup Egg Beaters omelet (mushrooms, green peppers) 1 slice wheat toast/1 teaspoon margarine if desired 1 cup skim milk	Open-faced tuna salad sandwich (1 slice bread; ½ cup tuna; chopped celery, green onions, mushrooms, low-calorie dressing) Low-calorie gelatin dessert/½ cup juice-packed fruit cocktail 1 cup skim milk	3 ounces roast turkey ½ cup mashed potatoes Cranberry sauce Asparagus Frozen yogurt bar (40 calories)
5	4 ounces grapefruit juice 1 egg, over easy 1 slice grain toast 1 cup skim milk	Turkey hot dog/1 slice bread; mustard, sauerkraut Cucumber vinaigrette salad Fresh fruit 1 cup skim milk	Beef kabobs (3 ounces lean beef; onions, mushrooms, green peppers, tomatoes) ½ cup rice ½ cup juice-packed fruit cocktail
6	½ cup canned peaches French toast (¼ cup Egg Beaters, ¼ cup skim milk, cinnamon, low-calorie syrup) ¾ cup skim milk	Open-faced roast beef sandwich (1 ounce roast beef; sprouts, tomatoes, 1 teaspoon mayonnaise) Fresh fruit 1 cup skim milk	3 ounces veal pizziola ½ cup spaghetti with sauce String beans Tossed salad/ low-calorie dressing Honeydew wedge

| 7 | ⅔ cup fresh strawberries 1 serving shredded wheat 1 cup skim milk | Legal pizza (½ English muffin, 1 slice part-skim mozzarella cheese, ½ cup tomato sauce) Carrot and celery sticks ½ cup fruit juice ice 1 cup skim milk | Chef salad (vegetables; 1 ounce turkey, 1 ounce turkey ham, 1 ounce Jarlsberg cheese); 1 tablespoon low-calorie dressing 5 RyKrisps Fresh fruit |

1,200-CALORIE DIET PLAN

BREAKFAST

4 ounces orange juice (or 1 serving of citrus fruit or juice from list)
*1 slice whole wheat toast (or other bread exchange)
Choose one of the following: 1 egg (limit 3 per week), ¼ cup Egg
  Beaters, 1 ounce part-skim milk cheese (limit 6 ounces per week),
  ½ cup low-fat cottage cheese, ⅓ cup (2 ounces) fish (if canned,
  must be water-packed), 1 tablespoon old-fashioned peanut butter
  (limit to 1 tablespoon daily)

LUNCH

Choose one of the following: 2 ounces fish or chicken (no skin), 1
  ounce turkey-based cold cuts (e.g., turkey ham), 1 ounce (slice)
  part-skim milk cheese, ½ cup low-fat cottage cheese, 1 cup skim
  milk yogurt, 1 tablespoon old-fashioned peanut butter
2 slices whole grain bread (or other bread exchange)
"A" vegetables (as desired)
1 fruit exchange

*Note: If you have only cereal and skim milk for breakfast, count the
cereal as a bread exchange and have an additional ounce of meat at
lunch or dinner.

DINNER

4 ounces fish, poultry (no skin), or veal; five times per week you may
  have 3 ounces of lean, well-trimmed beef, pork, ham, Canadian
  bacon, lamb, venison, rabbit, or shellfish (shrimp is limited to 3
  ounces per week)
1 small baked potato (or other bread exchange)
"A" vegetable (as desired)
½ cup "B" vegetable from exchange list
1 fruit exchange

Recommended daily: 2 cups skim milk or 2 skim milk exchanges.
Permitted daily: 1 fat exchange, 1 teaspoon low-sugar jam or jelly, and
  1 additional fruit exchange.

SAMPLE MEAL PLAN—1,200 CALORIES

Day	Breakfast	Lunch	Dinner
1	½ banana ¾ cup corn flakes 1 cup skim milk Coffee or tea	Turkey ham and cheese sandwich (2 slices wheat toast, 1 slice each turkey ham and Jarlsberg cheese; sprouts, lettuce, tomato, mustard and 1 tablespoon mayonnaise if desired) 1 apple 1 cup skim milk	5 ounces broiled halibut with lemon ½ cup carrots ½ cup herbed rice Tossed salad/low-calorie dressing ½ cup juice-packed pears
2	4 ounces orange juice 1 slice wheat toast 1 tablespoon legal peanut butter 1 cup skim milk	Assorted Relishes (celery, cucumber, carrot sticks) ½ cup low-fat cottage cheese ½ cup juice-packed pineapple 10 RyKrisps 1 cup skim milk	4 ounces pork chop/½ cup sage dressing ½ cup green peas Spinach salad ½ cup unsweetened applesauce

3	½ grapefruit 1 serving Oro wheat apple-cinnamon oatmeal 1 cup skim milk Coffee or tea	Cheese crisp (12-inch tortilla, 2 ounces part-skim cheese; tomatoes, green onions, chilies, lettuce, and 1 tablespoon guacamole, yogurt dip, or diet dressing) 1 peach 1 cup skim milk	4 ounces roast chicken (no skin) Broccoli Baked potato 1 teaspoon margarine Fresh fruit
4	Cantaloupe wedge ¼ cup Egg Beaters omelet (mushrooms, green peppers) 1 slice wheat toast/1 teaspoon margarine if desired 1 cup skim milk	Tuna salad sandwich (2 slices bread, ½ cup tuna; chopped celery, green onions, mushrooms, low-calorie dressing) low-calorie gelatin dessert/½ cup juice-packed fruit cocktail 1 cup skim milk	4 ounces roast turkey ½ cup mashed potatoes Cranberry sauce Asparagus Frozen yogurt bar (40 calories)
5	4 ounces grapefruit juice 1 egg, over easy 1 slice grain toast 1 cup skim milk	Turkey hot dog/1 slice bread; mustard, sauerkraut Cucumber vinaigrette salad Fresh fruit 1 cup skim milk	Beef kabobs (4 ounces lean beef; onions, mushrooms, green peppers, tomatoes) 1 cup rice ½ cup juice-packed fruit cocktail
6	½ cup canned peaches French toast (¼ cup Egg Beaters, ¼ cup skim	Roast beef sandwich (2 slices rye bread, 1 ounce roast beef; sprouts, tomatoes, 1 teaspoon mayonnaise)	4 ounces veal pizziola ½ cup spaghetti with sauce String beans Tossed salad/low cal-

	milk, cinna- mon, low- calorie syrup) ¾ cup skim milk	Fresh fruit 1 cup skim milk	orie dressing Honeydew wedge
7	⅔ cup straw- berries 1 serving shredded wheat 1 cup skim milk	Legal pizza (English muffin, 2 ounces part-skim milk moz- zarella cheese, ½ cup tomato sauce) Carrot and celery sticks ½ cup fruit juice ice 1 cup skim milk	Chef salad (vegeta- bles, 1 ounce turkey, 1 ounce turkey ham, 1 ounce Jarlsberg cheese); 1 teaspoon low-calorie dressing 5 RyKrisps Fresh fruit

One additional fruit exchange as a snack allowed daily.

1,400-CALORIE DIET PLAN

BREAKFAST

8 ounces orange juice (or 2 servings of citrus fruit or juice from list)
*2 slices whole wheat toast (or 2 bread exchanges)
Choose one of the following: 1 egg (limit 3 per week), ¼ cup Egg
  Beaters, 1 ounce part-skim milk cheese (limit 6 ounces per week),
  ½ cup low-fat cottage cheese, ⅔ cup (2 ounces) fish (if canned,
  must be water-packed), 1 tablespoon old-fashioned peanut butter
  (limit 2 tablespoons daily)

LUNCH

Choose one of the following: 3 ounces fish or chicken (no skin), 3
  ounces turkey-based cold cuts (e.g., turkey ham), 2 ounces (slices)
  part-skim milk cheese, 1 cup low-fat cottage cheese, 1 cup skim
  milk yogurt, 2 tablespoons old-fashioned peanut butter
2 slices whole grain bread (or other bread exchanges)
"A" vegetable (as desired)
1 fruit exchange

  *Note: If you have only cereal and skim milk for breakfast, count the
cereal as a bread exchange and have an additional ounce of meat at
lunch or dinner.

DINNER

5 ounces fish, poultry (no skin), or veal; three times per week you
  may have 5 ounces of lean, well-trimmed beef, pork, ham, Canadian bacon, lamb, venison, rabbit, or shellfish (shrimp is limited to 3 ounces per week)
1 small baked potato (or other bread exchange)
"A" vegetable (as desired)
½ cup of "B" vegetable from exchange list
1 fruit exchange

Recommended daily: 2 cups skim milk or 2 skim milk exchanges.
Permitted daily: 2 fat exchanges, 1 teaspoon low-sugar jam or jelly,
  and 2 additional fruit exchanges or 1 bread exchange.

SAMPLE MEAL PLAN—1,400 CALORIES

Day	Breakfast	Lunch	Dinner
1	1 banana ¾ cup corn flakes 1 slice wheat toast 1 tablespoon legal peanut butter 1 cup skim milk Coffee or tea	Turkey ham and cheese sandwich (2 slices wheat toast and turkey ham, 1 slice Jarlsberg cheese; sprouts, lettuce, to-mato, mustard, and 1 teaspoon mayon-naise if desired) 1 apple 1 cup skim milk	5 ounces broiled hal-ibut with lemon ½ cup carrots ½ cup herbed rice Tossed salad/low-calorie dressing ½ cup juice-packed pears
2	8 ounces or-ange juice 1 English muffin/1 teaspoon	Assorted Relishes (celery, cucumber, carrot sticks) 1 cup low-fat cottage cheese	5 ounces pork chop/½ cup sage dressing ½ cup green peas Spinach salad ½ cup unsweetened

margarine or jelly 1 cup skim milk	½ cup juice-packed pineapple 10 RyKrisps 1 cup skim milk	applesauce
3 ½ grapefruit 1 serving Oro wheat apple-cinnamon oatmeal 1 slice wheat toast 1 cup skim milk Coffee or tea	Cheese crisp (12-inch tortilla, 2 ounces part-skim cheese; tomatoes, green onions, chilies, lettuce, and 1 tablespoon guacamole, yogurt dip, or diet dressing) 1 peach 1 cup skim milk	5 ounces roast chicken (no skin) Broccoli Baked potato 1 teaspoon margarine Fresh fruit
4 Cantaloupe wedge ½ cup Egg Beaters omelet (mushrooms, green peppers) 1 slice wheat toast/1 teaspoon margarine if desired 1 cup skim milk	Tuna salad sandwich (2 slices bread, ½ cup tuna; chopped celery, green onions, mushrooms, low-calorie dressing) Low-calorie gelatin dessert/½ cup juice-packed fruit cocktail 1 cup skim milk	5 ounces roast turkey ½ cup mashed potatoes Cranberry sauce Asparagus Frozen yogurt bar (40 calories)
5 8 ounces grapefruit juice 1 egg, over easy 1 slice grain toast/1 teaspoon margarine	2 turkey hot dogs/2 slices bread; mustard, sauerkraut Cucumber vinaigrette salad Fresh fruit 1 cup skim milk	Beef kabobs (5 ounces lean beef; onions, mushrooms, green peppers, tomatoes) ½ cup rice ½ cup juice-packed fruit cocktail

	1 cup skim milk		
6	½ cup canned peaches 2 slices French toast (¼ cup Egg Beaters, ¼ cup skim milk, cinnamon, low-calorie syrup) ¾ cup skim milk	Roast beef sandwich (2 slices rye bread, 2 ounces roast beef; sprouts, tomatoes, 1 teaspoon mayonnaise) Fresh fruit 1 cup skim milk	5 ounces veal pizziola ½ cup spaghetti with sauce String beans Tossed salad/ low-calorie dressing Honeydew wedge
7	⅔ cup fresh strawberries ½ cup Egg Beaters, scrambled 1 slice wheat toast 1 cup skim milk	Legal pizza (English muffin, 2 ounces part-skim mozzarella cheese, ½ cup tomato sauce) Carrot and celery sticks ½ cup fruit juice ice 1 cup skim milk	Chef salad (vegetables, 2 ounces turkey, 1 ounce turkey ham, 1 ounce Jarlsberg cheese); 1 tablespoon low-calorie dressing Fresh fruit 5 RyKrisps

Two additional fruit exchanges or 1 bread exchange allowed daily.

Low-Calorie Snacking

As I have indicated earlier, snacking per se is not bad, nor is it an indication that you have gone off your diet. A little prudent nibbling may prevent you from inordinate gorging at meals. You already know that to lose weight is a matter of calorie adjustment—calories consumed versus calories burned—so there is no reason that sensible snacking cannot be worked into your overall diet plan.

The important consideration, however, is the *kind* of snacks you eat. They must be low in calories and you must not eat large portions. Remember to "bank" your snacks. If you know you want to eat two Oreo cream sandwich cookies, each at 50 calories, you will have to eliminate 100 calories from some other part of your daily food consumption. We have also suggested that you not buy snack food, but make your own instead. Treats that you make from scratch are safer for your diet because you know exactly what is in them.

Consult the following list of the more common snack foods for their calorie, protein, fat, and cholesterol contents. At the end of this list, we have included a sampling of low-calorie snacks that are better for you than the standard ones that most people munch on.

Calorie Values of Common Snack Foods

Food	Serving Size	Calories	Protein	Fat	Carbohydrates
Cakes and Cookies					
Angel food	¹/₁₀ cake	121	3.0	—	27.0
Brownies	2 x 2¾ inches	146	2.0	9	15.0
Chocolate cake (no icing)	2 x 3 x 2 inches	165	2.0	8	23.0
Chocolate icing	1 portion	38	—	1	8.0
Chocolate chip cookies	1	51	0.5	2	8.0
Chocolate sandwich cookies	1	99	1.0	5	13.0
Cupcake, plain, no icing	1	146	2.0	6	22.0
Oatmeal cookies	1	86	1.0	3	13.0
Oreo cream sandwich cookies	1	50	0.5	2	7.0
Pretzel	1	12	0.3	—	2.0

Pies

Cherry	¹/₆ of pie	418	4.0	18	61.0
Pecan	¹/₆ of pie	668	8.0	36	82.0

Candies

Caramel	1	42	—	1	8.0
Gumdrops	1 large	9	3.0	—	—
Jelly beans	10	66	—	—	17.0
Milk chocolate bar (Hershey's)	1 bar	302	5.0	19	32.0
Milky Way	1 bar	284	3.0	5	58.0

Beverages

Beer	12 ounces	171	2.0	—	16.0
Chocolate milkshake	8 ounces	421	11.0	18	58.0
Coca-Cola	12 ounces	156	2.0	—	41.0
Coffee, black	8 ounces	5	—	—	1.0
Diet 7-Up	12 ounces	4	—	—	1.0
Highball	8 ounces	166	—	—	—
Lemonade	8 ounces	104	0.2	—	27.2
Milk, chocolate	8 ounces	205	7.0	9	25.0
Milk, skimmed	8 ounces	81	8.0	—	12.0
Milk, whole	8 ounces	161	9.0	9	12.0
Pepsi-Cola	12 ounces	159	—	—	41.0
Tea, no sugar, no cream	8 ounces	2	—	—	0.4
Tom Collins	10 ounces	180	—	—	9.0

Miscellaneous

Carrot sticks, raw	3	13	0.4	—	3
Celery sticks	1	9	1.0	—	2
Cheese, cheddar	¾-inch cube	60	4.0	5.0	—
D-zerta gelatin	½ cup	10	2.0	—	—
French fries, ½ × ½ × 2 inches	10 pieces	137	2.0	7.0	18
Gelatin	⅔ cup	109	2.0	—	26
Graham crackers, 2½ × 2½ inches	1	30	5.0	1.0	5
Ice cream	⅔ cup	137	4.0	5.0	20
Olives, green	2 medium	15	—	2.0	—
ripe	2 large	37	—	4.0	1
Onion dip	1 tablespoon	31	1.0	3.0	2
Peanut butter	1 tablespoon	115	5.0	10.0	4
Pickles, sour	1 large	11	1.0	—	2
Popcorn, oil and salt added	1 cup	82	2.0	4.0	11
Potato chips, 2-inch diameter	5 chips	54	1.0	4.0	5
Ritz cracker	1	17	—	1.0	2
Saltine	1	14	—	0.4	2
Sherbet	⅔ cup	177	2.0	1.0	40

SOURCE: *Food Values of Portions Commonly Used*, Bowes and Church, 12th Edition.

Low-Calorie Snacks

Skim milk shake
Fruit juice ice
Frozen yogurt bar (40 calories)
Raw vegetables with hot sauce or dip
Pickles (not for low-sodium diets)
1 cup popcorn

½ cup Weight Watchers Ice Cream
6 ounces tomato or V-8 juice
Green been salad with low-calorie Italian dressing
½ cup D-zerta jello or pudding
½ cup diet gelatin fruit salad
½ cup juice-packed canned fruit
1½ full-size graham crackers
2-inch wedge angel food cake
Vegetable soup (chicken bouillon with your choice of "A" vegetables)

Losing Weight through Exercise

What role does exercise have in a weight-reduction program?

The answer, on paper, is quite simple. There is a classic formula for losing weight that has held true throughout the ages: The number of calories you burn up in daily activity must be *greater* than the number you consume in your daily meals. If you *burn as many* calories as you consume each day, you will maintain your present weight. If you *eat more* than you burn up, you will gain weight. The formula is simple. The hard part is to convert it into a program of diet and exercise that will show results where they count: in your mirror, on your bathroom scale, in the notches on your belt.

For years it was assumed that exercise played a minimal role in weight reduction. The amount of exercise needed to lose even one pound of weight seemed unrealistic for the average man and woman to work into a daily schedule of commitments that seemed more important than losing one pound. (We will look at this in a minute.) So emphasis was placed on diet, and since the diet had to reduce calories, most people interpreted diet to mean a greater degree of "hunger." Many diets for weight reduction consisted of nothing more than reducing the amount of food eaten. The result? Hunger pains, and not much weight loss. Since most people didn't want to be hungry for the amount of time it would take to lose a decent amount of weight, they quickly gave up.

Today we know that a person does not have to go hungry in

order to reduce. Overweight people do have to curb their eating and adjust their meals to include the right foods, as we have pointed out earlier, but exercise, as a key component in weight loss, reduces the necessity to rely soley on diet. In fact, coupled, diet and exercise can balance your weight-management efforts and speed up your weight loss.

How does exercise work in weight reduction?

If you want to lose one pound, you will have to burn up 3,500 calories. At first, this seems like an overwhelming task, especially when you consider that to burn up 100 calories you must walk or run one mile. (It makes no difference whether you walk or run. One mile requires 100 calories of energy to move the human body that distance. Of course, if you run it, you'll burn up the calories more quickly than someone who saunters along.) Next, with a little clever punching on your pocket calculator, you conclude that to lose one pound in a week would mean walking or running thirty-five miles in that week, and that divides up into five miles a day. If it were up to exercise alone, you might quickly conclude that there are more important and more fun things in life than doing five miles a day.

Now consider what will happen if you pair an aerobic exercise program with a low-calorie diet such as the one in this chapter. You could exercise to lose half your 3,500 calories a week. This would be 250 a day, instead of 500. In terms of miles, you would have to walk or run only 2.5 miles, which could be completed in less than an hour. While doing this, your diet plan lowers your caloric intake by 250 calories each day, and you still lose your one pound a week. At the Arizona Heart Institute we usually recommend that a person double these figures and most people find it quite reasonable to do so. By exercising 500 calories off each day (or enough sessions per week that it equals that amount) and reducing their meals by 500 calories, weight loss at about two pounds per week is more satisfying. If you can keep up this program for six months, you could lose roughly fifty pounds. That's not bad for a half year's effort!

Look what happens when you couple exercise and diet. When you cut back on your calories, your body's initial reaction is to suppose (we'll assume your body can think for the moment!) that you are going to starve. So it reduces its metabolism automatically and you begin to burn fewer calories. But when you start to exercise, your metabolic rate speeds up again. It's like tricking your body into thinking that you are not starving. So frequent exercise along with fewer calories consumed means greater weight loss.

Guidelines

Here are some pointers to help you begin a weight-management exercise program. You will need to read our chapter on exercise to supplement these guidelines.

1. Select an aerobic activity. Read about why aerobics are the best exercises for losing weight on page 195. Also use our section on exercise comparisons, beginning on page 208, to learn about the precautions that each type of exercise requires. Do not just begin running today!

2. Exercise at least three times or more each week. Frequency plays a major role in weight reduction. Two days of exercise will not meet the same energy expenditure or caloric cost as three days, even if the total mileage walked or run is the same.

3. Each exercise session should be at least thirty minutes long. When you first begin to work out, the energy you use comes from burning carbohydrates. What you want to burn up is energy stored in fat. Studies show that the first thirty minutes will not efficiently burn fat for significant weight loss. As your program progresses, prolonged exercise will cause fat to be used as a fuel source.

4. Follow a low-calorie diet so that you consciously eliminate about 500 calories a day from your regular meals.

5. Use the exercise/calorie exchange table below so you can balance your eating and exercising accurately around particular foods and activities. Apply the caloric "banking" procedures described earlier.

6. Study and apply the weight-management principles we have already given you. In this way your mental attitude will support your exercise efforts, and the psychological conditioning you need to stay on your diet will reinforce your commitment to exercise.

What to Expect

Marked improvements will be noticed in your daily living as you progress on your weight-management exercise program. The first six months will produce the most noticeable changes in your weight and body shape. Improvement, however, will come *gradually* during this period, so don't expect miracles overnight. Keep in mind that different people burn calories at different rates, so don't compare yourself with others who may be reducing with you. It is harder for some people to lose weight than it is for others. The important principle for everyone is to make sure he or she is expending more energy than is being stored in the body. If you follow this principle, you will lose weight.

Exercise Equivalents of Calories

FOOD	Weight (ounces)	Calories	Walking	Bicycling	Swimming	Jogging-Walking	Running
Alcoholic Beverages			(M I N U T E S)				
Beer (8 ounces)	8	240	22	18	14	12	6
Brandy (1 glass)	1	75	14	12	9	8	4
Daiquiri (1 glass)	3½	125	24	19	15	13	7
Martini (1 glass)	3½	140	27	22	16	14	8
Wine, burgundy (4-ounce glass)	4	110	21	17	13	11	6
Candy and Desserts							
Baby Ruth (1 ounce)	1	135	26	21	16	14	8
Hershey bar (1¼ ounces)	1¼	218	42	34	26	22	12
Chocolate chip cookies (3)	1	150	29	23	18	15	8
Fig Newtons (2)	1	110	21	17	13	11	6

Banana split	10	594	114	91	70	59	33
Eclair or cream puff	3½	296	57	46	35	30	16
Apple pie	5⅓	400	77	62	47	40	22

Cereal Products

Raisin bran, milk, sugar	5	212	41	33	25	21	12
Oatmeal, milk, sugar	10	260	50	40	31	26	14
Egg roll (vegetable)	1	66	13	10	8	7	4
Macaroni and cheese	7¼	505	97	78	59	51	28
Spaghetti and meatballs	7⅓	295	57	45	35	30	16
Taco (with beef)	2¹/₅	180	35	28	21	18	10

Fruits and Juices

Apple, raw	5	87	17	13	10	9	5
Apple, baked	5	188	36	29	22	19	10
Applesauce	3⅓	90	17	14	11	9	5
Orange Juice (4 ounces)	4	54	10	8	6	5	3

Meats and Poultry

Hamburger (3-inch patty)	2⁴/₅	224	43	34	26	22	12
T-bone steak	3	175	34	27	21	18	10
Stew	8	210	40	32	25	21	12
Frankfurter (no bun)	2	170	33	26	20	17	9
Veal roast	3	136	26	21	16	14	8
Fried chicken leg	1⅓	90	17	14	12	11	9
Turkey, dressing and gravy	7¼	448	86	69	53	45	25

Developed by Dr. Frank Konishi.

9 The Diet Factor

The expression "So-and-So's on a diet" reminds me of the way we say that "So-and-So's got a heart condition." Both of these expressions can be misleading because they seem to indicate something very exclusive. They seem to imply that only a select few are actually "on a diet" or that only the very sick have a "heart condition." You know from the results of your taking the Heart Test that you, too, have a "heart condition." We all do. Everyone's heart is in *some* condition. Fortunately, most of us have a good or acceptable "heart condition." But now is the time to consider that you, too, are already "on a diet." We all are. Unfortunately, many Americans are not on a very good diet. What is your personal diet? Who decides what it is?

You decide, and to a large extent you have already decided what your diet will be. You may not have done this as consciously as the person who begins a new diet and starts to restrict certain foods. Diets can be constructed unconsciously and they do not always restrict foods. If you drink six cans of cola a day, eat pizza once a week, never have breakfast, eat a burger from a fast-food diner three or four times a week for lunch, have a cocktail before dinner every evening, these are part of your diet—an unplanned, uncontrolled diet. The food you eat, the way you prepare it, the amounts you consume, the way your meals are balanced (or *not* balanced) with the four food groups, all of this constitutes your current diet. And just as conscious dieters hope that their diet will *do* something for them, so too does your diet *do* something for you. Diets *act* upon the dieter. They do something *to* you. Even your present diet, whatever it may be, is doing something to you. And to your heart.

This relationship between your diet and your heart may be a very intimate one. Countless studies and research experiments performed over the last thirty or forty years strongly suggest a positive correlation between the food you eat and the condition of your heart. This diet-heart theory was dramatically presented during World War II when the incidence of death from heart attacks among the population of Western Europe declined drastically while foods such as meat, dairy products, and eggs were curtailed because of wartime rationing. When hostilities came to an end and these food supplies once again became the daily fare, deaths from heart attacks began to increase. Curious about this, doctors and researchers began systematic studies into the adverse effect that these various foods have in the progression of atherosclerosis. Much of what we know today about heart care and diet therapy is a result of this research, and there is still much to discover.

Food and Your Heart

We at the Arizona Heart Institute believe that there is a direct relationship between certain types of food and atherosclerosis. Let's look at three primary ways that your heart is affected by the food you eat.

First, it is believed that cholesterol and triglycerides build up in the arteries of people whose blood carries elevated levels of these fats. Both of these substances are kinds of fat, much like apples and pears are kinds of fruit. Both these fatty elements are produced in the body, but you increase them when you eat certain foods. So your total cholesterol and triglyceride counts are derived from your own body's manufacture and the food you eat.

Second, a diet that is high in sodium can raise your blood pressure. Too much sodium in your body will cause you to retain fluids and this in turn increases your blood volume. Your heart must pump harder to cope with this and the extra force increases the pressure on the artery walls. The result is higher blood pressure.

Third, as you have learned from nagging TV commercials about diet soft drinks, excess calories mean excess pounds. Furthermore, foods that are high in fat are generally concentrated sources of calories. Being overweight is associated with hypertension, cardiovascular disease, diabetes, and other serious illnesses.

If you considered just these three risk factors—high blood fats, high blood pressure, and obesity—you would fall into the medium-risk category for heart complications. These three taken singly or in combination with each other are serious threats. So you can see that even though you may not consider yourself to be on a diet because you do not watch what you eat or restrict certain foods, you do have a diet—one high in cholesterol, sodium, and calories, a diet that may be contributing to the progression of atherosclerosis. In this chapter we will give you dietary advice to counteract the detrimental effects your eating habits may have on you. Specifically, we will show you how to change your eating habits so that your diet is low in fat and sodium. If you are overweight, you should begin the weight-management diet found in chapter 8.

Any diet—those we offer you here or the ones you've read about elsewhere—must be nutritionally balanced by incorporating foods from each of the four food groups. Every day you should have two servings of low-fat milk and dairy products, two servings from the high-protein group that includes eggs, poultry, fish, meat, beans, and legumes, three to four servings of whole grain breads or cereals, and four servings of fresh vegetables or fruit. In addition to this, you should plan your daily meals to be distributed along the following percentages: 55–60 percent of your daily food should be unrefined carbohydrates, 15–20 percent should be protein, and 20–25 percent should consist of fats.

Our nutritional approach closely parallels the United States dietary goals set up by the U.S. Senate Select Committee on Nutrition and Human Needs. Here are those goals that we believe best promote optimal health for you and your family:

1. You should strive to attain and then maintain your ideal weight. As you learned in our chapter on weight management

this can be done by balancing your caloric intake with output expended in physical activity. So diet and exercise, along with the behavioral and attitudinal changes that support them, are the core components to achieve your ideal weight.

2. You must eat carbohydrates. Your body needs a certain amount of sugar. You do *not* have to get your sugar allotment, however, from refined sugars that are found in so many commercial products on the market today. Instead eat more complex carbohydrates or foods that are sweet in their natural state. What foods are these? Fresh fruits and vegetables. Whole grain breads and cereals will also change to sugar in your body, so eat more of them as well.

3. The corollary to the preceding step is to actively and consciously reduce your consumption of refined and processed sugars. Go easy on table sugar, honey, jelly, candy, and other sugary products.

4. Fat contains highly concentrated amounts of calories, so you must reduce your overall fat intake. A good target to aim for is to get your fat consumption down to less than 25 percent of the total calories you eat each day.

5. Your cholesterol intake should be lowered to 300–500 milligrams a day; for example, limit liver, fatty meats, egg yolks.

6. Salt is 40 percent sodium. You should limit your intake of sodium by cutting down on the amount of table salt you use. Heavily salted foods should also be restricted, especially foods that are visibly salty, like potato chips and pretzels. Your target for sodium is to reduce the amount you consume to no more than 4 grams each day.

A diet that follows the basic guidelines we have outlined above can be very nutritious for you as well as good for your heart. If a diet does not provide your body with the nutrients it needs, it is a sham, no matter how it succeeds in changing your blood chemistry or making you lose weight. Americans are growing more diet conscious as they learn about the problems our sedentary way of life and our commercially processed foods are creating for us. In response, crafty diet wizards have appeared all over the country hawking what they claim are the latest dietary methods for nutritional eating. Be wary of them. Fad diets dupe innocent people into thinking, for example, that shedding unwanted pounds is easy, fun, and permanent. Other diets promise to cure atherosclerosis. Some promise you a longer life. In general, any diet that promises you a miracle is most likely a hoax. Don't believe diet instructors that claim you can "melt away" fat. Fat does not melt. Atherosclerosis doesn't "go away." You can spot a fad diet if it omits one or more of the essential food groups or emphasizes one to the exclusion of the others. A good example is the "grapefruit only" diet. You should also distrust a diet that reduces your drinking of fluids. Adequate fluids are necessary for optimal health no matter what kind of diet you are on. The human body always needs a certain amount of fluid to prevent dehydration.

A key element in any sound diet is knowledge. Know what you need, know what a particular diet is going to give you, know what it is going to deprive you of. Too many Americans, in spite of their sincere interest in the subject, are still quite ignorant about what makes a good diet and what makes a bad one. Too easily they are intrigued by the fad diets, the gimmicky food supplements, and the "natural" vitamin wonders on the market that promise a "new" you, but deliver the "old" you in much worse shape than when you began. Remember, a vitamin is no substitute for a sound diet. It is sad but true that many people have been hurt by these supposed cure-alls and wasted too much time and money in the process of harming their health. In recent years some popular diets, such as the Scarsdale, Beverly Hills, Stillman, and Atkins, have not educated the American public very well in the basics of sound nutrition. Some of these diets are dangerous and unbalanced. Some are difficult to follow. Some are boring. Most place too little or no emphasis on exercise and the life-style and attitudinal changes that must accompany a change in eating habits.

The dietary advice in this book is the product of years of treating patients with heart disease and other complicating factors that debilitate the cardiovascular system, such as overweight and high blood pressure. We know our diets are sound. We have seen living proof of their soundness in the patients who leave the Arizona Heart Institute healthier and happier than when they came to us. We do not promise "miracles" or claim to have the secret of "melting" away unwanted conditions. We are not miracle workers or "fat melters." We offer sound, practical advice incorporating the latest findings from well-controlled and respected studies in dietary research. We also include principles pioneered in older diet plans that have proven successful over the years.

We are also compromisers. We do not try to get you to change your eating style overnight. We know you have grown accustomed to the way you eat, and so we are happy if a person begins slowly to reduce the harmful foods in his or her diet. We never send a person home telling him or her to "go on a diet." Rather we ask people to adjust their present diets so that they eventually fall closer into line with diets that are safe and sound. For example, if you have been drinking a six-pack of beer each night for the last ten years and are today grossly overweight, our advice is not to stop drinking beer altogether. We will be happy if you reduce your nightly binge to four cans instead of six. Later, we will ask you to drop to three. Our belief is that small, permanent gains are infinitely better than large temporary ones. So what if you made it through the first evening without even one beer if by the following week you were back to a six-pack?

What's more, we believe that our diet plans offer you the widest variety of foods to make interesting, tasty meals. A diet pattern does not have to be dreadfully dull. Food should taste good. You will not stay with your diet very long if you approach mealtime without enthusiasm and find your meals day after day to be boring. We recognize the human dimension in food, the sharing of food with close friends and members of your family. The social element of meals must not be overlooked or you will not stay on your diet for life. You, your family, and your friends will enjoy our diet plans. Food should add years to your life, not shorten it. We cannot promise you a longer life with our diets, but I personally believe you will live longer, and you will certainly enjoy a better *quality* of life.

We have more recently learned that there are special circumstances in which our usual and customary dietary advice is inadequate. A select group of extremely high-risk patients are now participating in a program that includes the Diethrich Diet (see chapter 1). These patients with incurable cardiovascular disease have no other alternative. When they begin the Diethrich Diet, they begin it for a lifetime. It is one thing for a person to follow a diet for a month or two. It is another thing for you to readjust your eating habits so you persevere for the rest of your life. At the Arizona Heart Institute we take into account a patient's total life-style so that our diet may be personalized to fit that life-style for years after the patient leaves the initial program. We believe that proper values and attitudes are as nutritionally healthy for men and women's total well-being as the food they eat. Most of our patients recognize the wisdom of this, and, because of this personalized approach, we have been very successful in winning the dietary compliance of our patients after they leave the Institute.

In the preparation of this diet, we have studied numerous nutritional programs—for example, the Scarsdale and Atkins diets. Of particular interest to us has been the diet developed by Nathan Pritikin of California. Nathan and I have become acquainted over the past few years, and his staff and ours have participated together in programs on nutrition and diet. We initially tried the Pritikin diet for our highest-risk patients, and while there was little question about its effectiveness in lowering cholesterol, triglycerides, and blood sugar, we found that most patients, after their initial enthusiasm for the diet, tended to drift away and resort to many of their old eating habits. Since then, we have concluded that for many people his program turns out to be "impossible to follow" over the long haul. Since high-risk patients need to be on a diet the rest of their lives, it must be a "livable" diet. It must have variety. It must be interesting and surprising as well as nourishing. For example, foods that are high in cholesterol and saturated fats are very nutritious foods and they taste good. Most people look forward to favorite meals that include beef, cheese, and eggs. Unlike the Pritikin program, ours does not eliminate these foods altogether. We just cut them down to very small quantities and emphasize foods that are lower in cholesterol, such as chicken, fish, and tofu. Similarly, we do not restrict alcohol as stringently as does Pritikin, who allows only 4 ounces per week in cooking. We recognize that alcohol is a vasodilator, which is beneficial for people with atherosclerosis because it dilates the blood vessels, allowing the blood to flow more freely. Several studies have indicated that HDLs (the lipoproteins that prevent fatty deposits in the arteries) are higher in people who are moderate drinkers. By moderate we mean one to two drinks per day. We want our patients to anticipate the cocktail hour as a warm and relaxing moment in their busy day just as they used to do before they began the Diethrich Diet.

In contrast to the Pritikin theory, we do not emphasize that it is *total* cholesterol that is the most significant indicator of cardiovascular disease risk. From our own experience in Arizona, we are beginning to realize that it is the *ratio* of HDL cholesterol to total cholesterol that is the most reliable indicator. Therefore our approach is to get the total cholesterol level down throug diet and to raise HDLs through exercise and weight reduction.

Another point on which we disagree with Pritikin is his clai that by following his dietary plan, atherosclerosis will regress We have seen no human studies that confirm the theory tha atherosclerotic plaque will decrease by strict adherence to an diet. To our knowledge such evidence is not available, althoug it is certainly a goal to which all of us in research are aspirin We do feel that cardiovascular disease can be controlled b reducing those factors that contribute to atherosclerotic diseas Our program attempts to *control the progression of disease* s that it never gets to the point of triggering a serious heart attac or stroke. This is the best we can do at the present time. Th future is bright, however, and we look forward to the day whe atherosclerosis is fully understood and controlled. The Intern: tional Heart Foundation, which sponsors all of our research : the Arizona Heart Institute, has set that as our major goal.

The main focus of the Diethrich Diet is to improve the quali of life for our patients. In addition to the clinical data c cholesterol and triglyceride levels, stress tests on treadmill HDL counts, and blood pressure readings—all of which a extremely important indicators of a patient's health—we believ that the daily homelife, work experience, social commitment and recreational habits that our patients engage in are also acc rate indicators of health. In fact, without these, a person's tot health cannot be truly evaluated. The complete Diethrich Pr gram aims at mitigating the pain of cardiovascular disease ar the disabling effects it has on men and women, and then resto ing these high-risk individuals to a life-style they find norma invigorating, and satisfying.

Now let's look at diets for the specific abnormalities identifi in your Heart Test.

A Diet for People with Elevated Bloo Fats

What was your score on questions 7 and 8 on the Heart Tes If you scored higher than 0, it is because your cholesterol level elevated or because you have poor eating habits. Now it's tin to alter your diet to reduce the cholesterol and triglyceride leve in your blood. Both of these are fats that are elevated in the blood of people with certain kinds of heart disease. Both should be lowered into a safe range to reduce your chances of heart attack or stroke. Luckily, both these risk factors can be modified by diet, exercise, and weight reduction. The diet principles in this section were designed to lower these blood fats by reducing your intake of cholesterol, saturated fats, and refined carbohydrates or simple sugars. What are these three elements found in so many foods and what do they do to us?

Cholesterol

Cholesterol is necessary for life. It is an essential component in all our cells and provides a chemical base that produces certain hormones and vitamin D. Where does it come from? Most of the cholesterol in your body was produced internally, in your liver. Some of the cholesterol you ingested through the food you ate. Your total cholesterol level is a composite of these. There is also a hereditary factor involved that regulates the amount of cholesterol your body produces naturally. Some people produce more cholesterol; others excrete more. But almost everyone can reduce their overall cholesterol count by reducing the amount of cholesterol eaten. Since cholesterol is present only in animal fats, these are the foods that need to be watched. Foods of plant origin do not have cholesterol, but some contain coconut and palm oils, which are saturated fats (see below). By a carefully structured diet, low in cholesterol, you will be assisting your body in balancing its cholesterol level and thereby inhibiting the further progression of atherosclerosis by eliminating one of the key ingredients in atherosclerotic plaque. We do not advocate diets that completely eliminate cholesterol because foods that contain it are very nutritious and your body needs them. Our method is simply to set limits on the amount you eat and substitute other foods lower in cholesterol.

Fats

What are fats good for, anyway?
Well, for one thing, they taste good. Most of us have a natural craving for the flavor of fat. They do add a mouthwatering dimension to foods. It is very satisfying to eat fat because it

produces that feeling of fullness after a meal. It takes longer for your stomach to digest fat than any other food, so you feel full longer after a meal that includes fat. You may notice sometimes when you eat a meal comprised of nothing but vegetables, fruit, bread, and very lean meat how quickly you get hungry after the meal is over. Like Cantonese food, these meals just do not stick to your ribs very long. Biochemically, fats supply you with an essential fatty acid and transport fat-soluble vitamins through your body.

The *important point to remember about fats* is that, although we need some fat, it occurs naturally in a wide variety of foods, so the chances of your getting what you need are very good without adding extra fat to your meals. *Keep the fat content of your diet as low as possible*. When you do add fat, as in cooking, use polyunsaturated fats. These will lower your cholesterol levels rather than increase them. You need not fear using small amounts of polyunsaturated fats in your cooking. You can recognize them because they remain in an oily liquid state at room temperature.

Saturated fats, on the other hand, tend to raise the level of cholesterol in the bloodstream. A saturated fat is usually any thick, heavy· fat that is in a solid or semisolid state at room temperature. Many food manufacturers add quantities of saturated fats to their products because they increase the shelf life of certain foods, preventing them from going bad. Saturated fats are also cheaper for this purpose than other preservatives. You must read the labels of the products you buy very carefully to see how much saturated fat is in them. You can reduce the amount of saturated fat you consume by avoiding animal fats, shortening, coconut oil, palm oil, and hydrogenated fat or hardened vegetable oil. In general, you want to keep your diet as low in total fat as possible, so read labels carefully for these other forms of it. Sometimes manufacturers fool you into thinking their brands are safe by telling you that they contain no cholesterol. But if they have replaced it with hydrogenated fat, for example, they have defeated their purpose in attempting to render their products safe. Certain brands of peanut butter are notorious for this. Read their labels and compare them with "old-fashioned style" peanut butter that contains nothing but peanuts and salt.

Refined Carbohydrates

These are simple sugars. You find them in table sugar, honey, fructose, and desserts made with them. Like fats, they taste good and some people's craving for them borders on obsession. Their sweet tooth is constantly on edge. Unfortunately refined sugars are also culprits in heart disease by raising triglycerides in the blood, not to mention their other subversive activities that contribute to tooth decay, obesity, and diabetes. In our efforts to promote your optimal health, we limit these types of food in our diet. If you have a highly elevated triglyceride level, fasting blood sugar, or you are diabetic, we recommend *complete avoidance* of sugars, along with a strict limitation on alcoholic beverages. The reason for alcoholic limitations is not because of any directly adverse reaction or effect on the heart, but rather the fact that alcohol is high in carbohydrates, which convert to triglycerides if consumed in excess. Mixed drinks with cola, tonic, or ginger ale compound the problem even more. So on our diet, to be really safe we recommend no more than two drinks a day.

Twenty-four Ways to Make Your Diet Low in Cholesterol, Saturated Fat, and Refined Carbohydrates

Here are some principles you can apply to lower the cholesterol, saturated fat, and refined carbohydrates in your diet.

1. You may not be able to pull your sweet tooth, but you will have to tame it. Avoid the following: sugar, honey, corn syrup, marmalade, molasses, candy, fructose, frosting, regular type jam, regular type jelly, regular type pancake syrup, and other very sugary foods and desserts.
2. Artificial sweeteners may be like "fool's gold" to fill your sweet tooth. But use them moderately because there is still considerable controversy over their long-term effects. If you use them long enough, you may actually get to like them. Some people claim that they would never go back to regularly sugared soft drinks because of taste alone. Sugar-free pop, jelly, jam, preserves, gum, and syrup certainly

reduce your sugar intake, but moderation is advised until better studies on their effects are concluded.

3. Milk and dairy products that have had the fat skimmed off are best. They may be "skim" but you don't have to skimp. Some are labeled "nonfat" because all fat has been removed. Those labeled "low fat" have had only half the fat removed.

4. No processed cheese, please. And no squeeze cheese. Eat only 3 ounces of regular type cheese per week. You can double it to 6 ounces if part of the cheese is the skim type.

5. When it comes to eggs, you may be in the habit of breaking the yoke. Well, now you will have to break the yolk habit. Limit yourself to three egg yolks a week. This includes those used in cooking or those already present in foods. You can have as many egg whites as you desire.

6. Beef up your meals with less beef. Try fish, veal, tofu, and chicken that has been skinned.

7. Red meat should be eaten rare(ly). You must not eat more than one pound per week of beef, pork, lamb, venison, or rabbit.

8. When you purchase a cut of meat, cut some more. Specifically, cut off all visible fat before preparing. If you buy the leaner cuts to begin with, you won't have so much to trim. Cooking meat without its fat can sometimes dry it out, but if you keep it covered for a long period of time in a liquid or with a tenderizer it should stay moist and tender.

9. Really cut down the amounts of organ meats, such as liver, heart, and kidney. They are too rich in cholesterol. However, if you do not eat egg yolks, you can trade off each egg yolk for 2 ounces of organ meat.

10. All fatty meat and processed meat are to be avoided because, among other things, you may get fat in the process. These include: bacon, sausage, corned beef, and pastrami. Also avoid all luncheon-type meat, such as bologna, salami, and frankfurters. For a change of pace, check out the turkey-based products, such as ham, bologna, and frankfurters.

11. You will have to skimp on shrimp. Most shellfish is permitted, but shrimp must be limited to 3 ounces and eaten only two to four times a month.

12. Safflower, sunflower seed, walnut, corn, soybean, cotton-seed, and sesame oil may all sound like exotic fragrances or mysterious potions, but they are just fat. And these fats you may use for cooking because they are the polyunsaturated fats, but keep your total fat intake low.

13. From now on when the waiter or waitress asks you what type of dressing you want on your salad, you won't have to think so hard. Choose oil-based salad dressings, such as Italian or French. Avoid creamy types, like blue cheese and Roquefort. Naturally, the low-calorie and no-oil types contain less fat and are a better choice. Order salad dressing on the side so that you can determine how much you use.

14. The world seems saturated with fats, especially saturated fats. Here is the long list of them: any solid fat, hardened oils or fats, shortening, lard, suet, butter, cream cheese, bacon fat, meat drippings containing fat, coconut oil, palm oil, cocoa butter, sweet cream, sour or whipped cream. Coffee cream substitutes, artificial sour creams, and whipped toppings usually contain coconut oil, palm oil, or other saturated fats and are best avoided.

15. Some margarines come in tubs for a reason. It's not just so you can save the plastic container for leftovers. These margarines are soft usually because they contain a liquid polyunsaturated oil as the main ingredient (and therefore listed first on the label). You should buy these tub types.

16. Sticking your meat on a spit and letting it drip over an open fire may sound primitive, but it is one of the best ways to cook meat to reduce the total fat. Baking, broiling, and barbequeing all reduce the total fat better than frying foods in their own grease. Avoid commercially fried foods since they retain a lot of their fat.

17. Nuts! Yes, they are high in fat. Eating nuts in moderation, however, is both permissible and a contradiction in terms. But if you can do it, do it. Do not eat cashew, Brazil, and macadamia nuts. When you buy peanut butter, get the "old-fashioned type" that contains just peanuts and salt. The preservatives in the "newfangled" style are saturated fats.

18. When you hear the call, "Soup's on!" hope that it is broth-based rather than cream-based. If you see any fat or grease on the surface, skim it off if possible.

19. Everyone needs a chocolate "fix" now and then, but you'll have to find substitutes. Chocolate is cocoa and butterfat. Unsweetened cocoa is acceptable. Carob powder is, too, but the commercial brands of carob candy bars generally contain coconut or palm oil. If you are a "chocoholic," you may have to try more drastic measures.

20. What's for dessert? Not very much on this diet. It is best to limit yourself to one dessert a day or even less. Any dessert is okay if it is made from recommended ingredients. Fruit juice ice, angel food cake, and graham crackers are acceptable.

21. There is a wide variety of fresh fruits and vegetables to enhance our meals. American society is so meat-oriented that we really have not explored all the possibilities of using them as major food items. On your diet, you should eat plenty of fruits and vegetables. Avocados and olives, however, should be used in moderation because they are high in fat. If you buy canned fruit, rinse it thoroughly to remove the syrup. It is preferable to purchase the juice- or water-packed varieties because they are not drowned in sugary syrup.

22. De-emphasize the use of fatty meats in your main meal. Restaurant menus have brainwashed us into thinking that entrees must generally be meat. Unrefined carbohydrates can replace meat. These include whole grain breads, unsweetened cereals, potatoes, pasta, rice. Turn meat into a side order or use it to add flavor to, rather than be, the main course.

23. What will you have to drink? Well, you should consult with your physician regarding the use of caffeine and alcohol. Remember, caffeine is contained in some foods, like those that have cocoa in them. Alcohol is not forbidden on our diet, but you should limit yourself to one or two drinks a day. One drink would be the equivalent of 3 to 4 ounces wine, one light beer, 1 ounce hard liquor.

24. Read labels carefully. Familiarize yourself with the label-reading techniques later in this chapter. If the manufacturer does not specify what type of oil was used, don't buy it. Remember, cholesterol is found only in animal fats, but there are several vegetable oils and vegetable fats that are saturated and these will raise cholesterol levels. Unfortunately, manufacturers often take advantage of this and

mislead the consumer into buying a product that is not permissible. An example of this would be a food label that states "made with 100 percent vegetable shortening." First of all, the label does not specify which vegetable oil is used, and second, shortening is a saturated fat.

As we told you earlier, it is okay to snack on the diets we advocate at the Arizona Heart Institute. Snacking in itself is not bad for you. In fact, there is evidence that people who nibble regularly may eat better than the gorgers who wolf it down at one sitting. The problem, of course, is that we snack either on the wrong foods or at the wrong times. But it is a normal urge to get a bit hungry between meals or after some physical activity and want a bite to eat. So, here is a list of acceptable snacks that will not ruin your diet. And, if you eat them at reasonable times of the day, they will not spoil your appetite either.

Acceptable Snacks

Skim milk
Low-fat cottage cheese or other low-fat cheese
Dips made with low-fat cottage cheese or skim milk yogurt
Old-fashioned-style peanut butter (contains no added fat)
Raw vegetables with hot sauce, low-fat cottage cheese
Fresh, or juice- or water-packed canned, fruit or juice
Popcorn popped with no fat or polyunsaturated oil
Legal potato chips or corn tortilla chips
Shakes made with skim milk, fruit or fruit juices and ice cubes
Pickles
Fruit *juice* ices (preferably homemade)
Frozen, *skim milk* yogurt bars (40 calories)
Low-calorie gelatin desserts
Graham crackers or vanilla wafers
V-8 or tomato juice
Angel food cake
Dried fruit (Use Weight Watchers brand if counting calories)
Skim or low-fat yogurt flavored with extract and sweeteners

Eating Out

People on a special diet often refuse to eat out for fear of going off the diet, or they go off it on occasions when they do eat out and justify it to themselves by claiming it is too hard to stay on a diet when you eat out. Neither has to be the case. You can eat out *and* you can stick to your diet. In our chapter on weight management we give you some ways to cope with restaurants, waiters, waitresses, menus, and, of course, your friends who are going to order all the mouth-watering foods that you aren't allowed. Here are some hints for staying faithful to your low-cholesterol, low-saturated-fat, and low-refined-carbohydrate diet.

1. A hearty appetizer, gazpacho soup, or a salad before the main course of the meal will help cut down the amount of meat you will eat at the meal. In fact, sometimes why not just make your entire meal from the appetizer and salad sections of the menu?

2. Order à la carte. This way your plate won't come loaded down with a food you don't want or with grease running into the vegetables.

3. Put yourself first in restaurants. Pretend that the old slogan "The customer is always right" is true. Ask for what you want. Remember, you can give the cook specific cooking instructions. Send word back to use no salt or fat. Most restaurants stay in business by pleasing the customer!

4. Meals low in sugar, cholesterol, and saturated fat are available on airplanes. This goes for low-sodium meals, too. So if your flight includes a meal, request one low in cholesterol and saturated fat when you make your reservations. Do this at least twenty-four hours in advance of the flight departure date.

5. Many restaurants serve low-cholesterol egg substitutes at breakfast, margarine, skim milk, and low-calorie syrup upon request. Call before going just to make sure.

6. Oriental restaurants are permitted once in a while. They use peanut oil for their fried foods, though, so order a steamed vegetable meal that does not include rich sauces. If you are watching your blood pressure, order meals without MSG or

soy sauce. It doesn't matter whether you eat with plastic or wooden chopsticks. Both are permitted.

7. Mexican restaurants serve food that contains much cholesterol and saturated fat. Order dishes that are not fried, and are made with lean meats; for example, chicken enchilada, taco, soup, salad. Mexican hot sauce is permitted.

In addition to these general hints, we like to give our dieters some suggestions on what to order from menus. You will see from the wide variety of food that you are permitted to select that your special diet need not cause you any great inconvenience or take the pleasure out of dining out. You will still be able to order delicious and healthful meals. Here are our suggestions organized around breakfast, lunch, and dinner.

Breakfast

Fruit or juice. Select any fresh fruit on the menu. Be careful about canned fruits, as they are usually packed in syrup. Make sure that they are juice- or water-packed.

Cereal. Usually hot or cold cereal is a good choice. Ask first when selecting hot cereals to see if whole milk was added in preparation.

Eggs. Follow the limit of three egg yolks per week. Whites may be eaten as desired. There are restaurants that serve low-cholesterol egg substitutes for breakfast. Occasionally, substitute lean Canadian bacon for eggs.

Breakfast bread. Skip the French toast, sweet rolls, and doughnuts in favor of English muffins, bagels, or commercial loaf bread such as enriched white, whole wheat, or rye. Firmly request that these not be buttered and, instead, that margarine be served at the table.

Beverage. Request skim or low-fat milk for cereal. Coffee, tea, or decaffeinated coffee is fine to order. Avoid restaurant coffee creamers if they contain saturated fat or if you do not know what type of fat they contain; use skim or low-fat milk.

Lunch

Soup. Soups are generally quite salty. Occasionally you may choose clear soups such as bouillon or consommé or broth-based vegetable-type soups. Skim off any visible fat. Gazpacho is a good choice, as it is low in sodium and fat. Avoid cream soups.

Sandwiches. Good choices are those made with chicken, turkey, tuna fish, or lean meat. Charbroiled or barbecued hamburgers are permitted. Mayonnaise, mustard, catsup, horseradish, pickles, onions, lettuce, and tomato may be included. Avoid cold cuts and hot sandwiches with gravy. Specify that no salt be added in food preparation.

Salad. A chef salad or spinach salad is a nice change. Make sure that you ask what the ingredients are and ask the waiter to substitute turkey or lean meat for luncheon meat, bacon, or cheese. Taking advantage of the salad bar is a good choice. You can pick and choose the ingredients. Order salad dressing on the side so that you can determine how much you use.

Dinner

Appetizer. Select vegetable juice, fruit juice, melon, or raw vegetables such as carrot and celery sticks.

Entree. Choose roasted, broiled, or barbecued entrees such as lean beef, shellfish, or pork in small portions. Fish, turkey, or chicken without gravy and with the skin removed are excellent choices. Avoid breaded or fried meats and do not eat any visible fat. It is a good idea to order meat broiled specifically without butter and salt because many restaurants make a practice of heaping a generous pat of butter on meats before broiling.

A chef, spinach, or fresh fruit salad can be an alternate selection.

Vegetables. Choose plenty of vegetables but try to avoid those cooked with salt, butter, or served in a cream sauce. If you must, ask for margarine but not butter for your baked potato. If margarine is not available, then eat it with hot sauce, chives, and pepper, or just plain.

Salad. A tossed salad made of lettuce, tomatoes, carrots, cabbage, green onions, and other raw vegetables is a perfect choice as are fresh fruit salads.

Specifically ask for an oil-based salad dressing such as French or Italian, or use vinegar, vinegar and oil, or lemon juice as a salad dressing.

Bread. French, Italian, whole wheat, and commercial loaf breads, Melba toast, or crackers are good selections. Avoid salty items and specialty breads in which shortening is used in preparation, such as biscuits. Ask for margarine in place of butter.

Dessert. Choose fruit such as melon or strawberries without cream, sherbet, angel food cake, or gelatin.

Beverage. Your usual coffee, tea, decaffeinated coffee, or Postum is good to order. When choosing alcoholic beverages, avoid those made with coconut, milk, or presweetened mixes (for example, piña coladas, frozen daiquiris, rum and cola). Order Margaritas without salt.

How to Read Labels

A skill you need to assure success with your diet is "label reading." Learn how to read labels and choose the best products for your diet. Here are some handy rules.

1. Most packaged foods are required to have a list of ingredients on the label, with the ingredient in the largest amount *listed first*. The ingredient present in the least amount is listed last.

2. It is wise to avoid buying items that are not clearly labeled, such as those that warn you ambiguously that the product is "made with one or more of the following oils."

3. Check to see if the product contains ingredients not allowed on your diet that might be concealed in "preservatives, flavorings, or other food additives."

4. Check the dietetic or low-sodium section of your grocery store for diet aids. Health food stores also offer a wide variety of acceptable foods.

5. When reading the ingredient list, check the meat, dairy product, egg, and fat content of a product. The chart on pages 170 and 171 will show you how to compare and choose products wisely.

6. Do not assume that if a product is labeled "low fat" that it is acceptable. Read the label carefully. It may be low in *total* fat content, but what fat it does contain may be saturated fat. The same applies to food labeled as "dietetic" or "nondairy."

7. Do not assume that because one food product of a company is acceptable for your diet all other products of the same company are also acceptable. Read and evaluate every label.

8. Occasionally reread the labels on products you have been purchasing. Companies change their ingredients now and then.
9. When purchasing products that contain fat, choose those food items that specify *"liquid"* polyunsaturated oil. If a label reads "vegetable fat," "vegetable shortening," or "vegetable oil," this usually means it is made of coconut oil, palm oil, or other saturated fats that you want to avoid. If you cannot avoid purchasing a product that contains some hydrogenated or hardened fat, then try to select the type that has the saturated fat listed as far as possible toward the end of the ingredient list.

Label Examples

The following are examples of labels you will find on commonly purchased products. They will give you a guideline to selecting between various brands of the same type of product. The key ingredients to check are *italicized*.

Margarine

GOOD CHOICE

Liquid corn oil, partially hydrogenated soybean oil, water, salt, *nonfat dry milk,* artificial flavor and color

Polyunsaturates—5 grams
Saturates—2 grams

POOR CHOICE

Partially hardened soybean oil, liquid corn oil, water, salt, *nonfat dry milk,* artificial flavor and color

Polyunsaturates—3 grams
Saturates—2 grams

Fish

GOOD CHOICE

Tuna, water, and salt

POOR CHOICE

Tuna, *oil*, and salt

Cake Mix

GOOD CHOICE

Cake flour, sugar, *liquid vegetable oil, cocoa,* dried *egg whites, skim milk solids,* starch, baking powder, salt, vanillin, and BHT

POOR CHOICE

Enriched flour, sugar, *shortening, milk,* leavening, dextrose, artificial flavors, salt, dried *sour cream,* corn starch, *egg,* BHA, and BHT

Pudding Mix

GOOD CHOICE

Sugar, dextrose, cornstarch, *cocoa* processed with alkali, salt, emulsifier, and artificial flavor

POOR CHOICE

Sugar, dextrose, cornstarch, *milk, chocolate,* salt, emulsifier, and artificial flavor

Peanut Butter

GOOD CHOICE

Peanuts and salt

POOR CHOICE

Peanuts, *shortening,* and salt

A Diet for People with High Blood Pressure

How did you rate on the blood pressure question on the Heart Test, question 9? If you rated high, that is, a 5 or 10, you are at definite risk for heart and blood vessel disease. A major component in our treatment for the hypertensive person is a dietary program, particularly as it relates to salt.

Americans eat too much salt, and in the process we consume too much sodium. On the average we consume about 8 to 15 grams of sodium a day, while the National Academy of Sciences advises that humans need only about half a gram a day. An inordinate amount of this excess sodium comes from ordinary table salt, which is 40 percent sodium. Even in tropical climates, some cultural groups live healthy lives with as little as half a gram of sodium a day in spite of the hot temperatures and the profuse sweating that we in America associate with the need for salt supplementation. At one time it was considered prudent to take salt tablets during hot summer weather, but more recently we have been warned against it. The human need for sodium is not as great as we may have previously thought. Nevertheless, sodium is a necessary mineral that must be in our daily diet because it is necessary for life. Our problem, however, is not that we might get too little of it, but that we overload ourselves with it by using a food item daily with a very high concentration of this essential mineral.

Why do we eat so much salt? Because we have *learned* to like salty food. Some cultures do not salt their food as extensively as we do. Consequently, for them high blood pressure is a rare phenomenon. Also, people who have not been reared on a high-salt diet do not find their meals "tasteless" because they lack salt. On the other hand, many Americans claim that unsalted food is precisely that—tasteless. Of course they don't say that they can't taste anything! The way they put it is that salt "brings out the flavor." And it does—for us. Cultural groups that are not as salt-happy as we are can taste the flavor of food without salt.

Salt and Your Heart

What does sodium do in terms of your heart? Excessive amounts of sodium cause our bodies to retain fluids, excessive amounts of fluid that we would ordinarily eliminate in the normal course of the day. This excess fluid overloads your vascular system, placing an extra work load on the heart. Simultaneously, your blood pressure increases. So by reducing the amount of salt you use, you can reduce the amount of sodium you take in and control your elevated blood pressure. As you know from the Heart Test, by decreasing the risk factor of high blood pressure, you lower your chances of suffering a heart attack or stroke.

At first your meals may taste "funny" when you decrease the amount of salt in them. You are used to the familiar taste that salt adds to your meals. But keep in mind that liking salty food is an *acquired* taste, one you learned over many years and, given time, you can unlearn it. Even better, start your children on diets low in sodium so that by the time they reach your age, one of the potential risk factors for heart disease will already be eliminated. You might say that you can "shake" the salt habit. Clever cooks will learn how to use other flavoring techniques to replace salt, and your meals will not taste as bland as you might suppose. Later in this chapter we will show you the spice and herb substitutions that will reeducate your tastebuds so they will enjoy meals with less salt.

How to Lower the Sodium in Your Diet

You are already "on a diet." If you have high blood pressure, here are some general principles that will lower the amount of sodium that you now ingest in your present diet.

1. Resist the urge to say, "Pass the salt, please." You really do not need to salt your food beyond the preparation stage. If you really must add salt at the table, use only about half a teaspoon each day. If you watch people around you while they are eating, you'll notice how many "salt abusers" there are in this world. They immediately reach for the salt and shake it vigorously over their food even before they taste it. Become a taster and a tester. Don't assume that all food sitting on a plate in front of you needs salt. Try it first.

2. This may kill your Happy Hour, but you should leave the salt off your Margaritas and stay away from the bowls of chips and dips. Most chips have salt on them. In fact Happy Hour is notorious for luring us into a salt-fest. Potato chips, corn chips, pretzels, salted nuts, and salted crackers must be avoided. In general, avoid any food that has salt visible on it. If you can see it, flee it. Substitute instead fresh vegetables and an appropriate dip that contains little salt.

3. Did you even suspect Dagwood of having high blood pressure? Not only does hypertension reign in the Bumstead household, but the master's famous mile-high sandwiches packed with luncheon meat do nothing to eliminate it. You

should scale down the contents of your own sandwiches t
the bare minimum. Avoid processed cheese. If you mus
have lunch meat, eat only four slices of turkey-based ham
salami, franks, or bologna a week. Yes, a week. Not pe
sandwich.

4. Fresh or canned unsweetened fruit and fruit juice each da
is allowed. Buy canned fruit that is packed in its ow
juices or in water. If it is not, then rinse it first to remov
the syrup.

5. Not all soups are "mmmm-mmmmmgoood." Not for you
Avoid the commercial soups and make your own. Home
made soup without salt and fat is okay.

6. Vegetables are a dieter's delight. You can eat as many o
them as you wish. Remember not to add salt to them afte
they are prepared. Some canned vegetables come pickle
in salt brine. Sauerkraut, olives, and pickles are goo
examples. Avoid them.

7. Do not use softened water. It may be soft but it is no
harmless. When the people who make softened water tak
the hard minerals out, they replace them with sodium.

8. Limit commercial salad dressing, catsup, and chili sauce t
one tablespoon daily. Regular tomato juice or V-8 juice i
limited to a half cup per day.

9. Most diet soda has quite a bit of sodium in it even though i
is low in calories. It has to have something in it! So limi
yourself to two cans per day. Diet Pepsi and Diet Rite Col
have a lower sodium content, so you may quench you
thirst with these two more frequently.

10. American science is great for coming up with artificia
substitutes for things we aren't supposed to have. There ar
salt substitutes on the market, but you should check wit
your physician about them. Avoid light salt. Also, some o
the over-the-counter antacids, like Alka-Seltzer, are high i
sodium. Ask your doctor or your nutritionist which are bes
for you.

11. If you are cooking with garlic, onion, or celery seasonings
do not use the flavored salts. You can buy the powder
instead.

12. Here is a list for you gourmet cooks who may have to limi
the amount of salt you can use. You don't have to give u
fancy dishes because of your diet. As you can see from th
list below, there are quite a few condiments, herbs, an

spices that are allowed. There are also special cookbooks available on how to cook with them. In time, you will probably not miss your meals seasoned in your former way.

CONDIMENTS

ALLOWED

Allspice	Garlic—fresh	Oregano	Sesame seeds
Aniseed	or powder	Paprika	Sorrel
Basil	Horseradish	Parsley	Tarragon
Bay leaves	root	Pepper—black,	Thyme
Caraway seeds	Juniper	red, or white	Turmeric
Cardamom	Lemon juice	Pimiento	Vinegar
Chili powder	Mace	Poppy seeds	
Chives	Marjoram	Poultry sea-	
Cinnamon	Mint	soning	
Curry powder	Mustard	Purslane	
Dill	Nutmeg	Rosemary	
Extracts such as	Onion—fresh,	Saffron	
almond or va-	juice, or pow-	Sage	
nilla	der	Savory	

AVOID

Bouillon cubes
Celery salt
Garlic salt
Horseradish, prepared
MSG (monosodium gluta-
mate)
Olives
Onion salt
Pickle relishes and other re-
lishes

Pickles
Sea salt
Soy sauce
Steak sauce
Table salt
Teriyaki sauce
Worcestershire sauce

Now you can see why our patients at the Arizona Heart Institute are so receptive to our nutritionist's recommendations and dietary advice. Limiting the amount of salt you use does not have to be unduly burdensome. You can still enjoy hearty and healthy meals.

Here are some ways to season your meals without salt if you are on a low-sodium diet.

Seasoning Suggestions for Low-Sodium Diets

Where no recipes are available, start with about ¼ teaspoon of spice or dried herbs to each pound of meat, or one pint of sauce or soup. Make this ⅛ teaspoon in the case of red pepper or garlic powder.

You will enjoy developing your own flavor combinations but try the following suggestions first:

Beef. Dry mustard, marjoram, nutmeg, sage, thyme, pepper, bay leaf, basil, caraway seed, curry, dill, rosemary, savory, onion, garlic.

Roast Beef—rub with pepper and ginger.

Goulash—cook with onion, bay leaf, tomato, paprika, pepper, rosemary or oregano and bitters.

Pork. Sage, basil, caraway seed, thyme, marjoram, rosemary, chives, onion, garlic; serve with unsweetened applesauce or spiced apples.

Lamb. Mint, rosemary, curry, dill, whole cloves, sage, marjoram, garlic, onion; serve with unsweetened broiled pineapple rings. Rub *chops* with pepper and ginger before broiling.

Veal. Bay leaf, ginger, marjoram, curry, basil, savory, thyme, garlic, onion; serve with unsweetened apricots. Rub *chops* with pepper and saffron.

Veal Stew. Cook with onion, bay leaf, powdered mace, celery leaves and bitters.

Chicken. Paprika, thyme, sage, parsley; serve with unsweetened cranberry sauce.

Fish. Dry mustard, paprika, curry, bay leaf, lemon juice, lemon, and margarine.

Eggs. Pepper, dry mustard, paprika, curry, green pepper, onion; serve omelet with unsweetened pineapple.

Asparagus. Lemon juice, French dressing, grated nutmeg.

Beans, Green. Marjoram, lemon juice, nutmeg, French dressing, dillweed, onion.

Cabbage. Mustard dressing, dillweed, margarine with lemon, vinegar.

Carrots. Parsley, margarine, mint, nutmeg, tarragon, chives.

Cauliflower. Nutmeg, bitters.

Corn. Green pepper, tomatoes, freshly ground black pepper.

Cucumber. Raw, sliced thin with onion rings in vinegar.

Eggplant. Peel, dice, boil and drain; add tomatoes, bay leaf, and oregano.

Squash. Onion, ginger, mace.

Peas, Green. Mint, parsley, onion.

Onion. Boil with clove and thyme.

Tomatoes. Broil with margarine; stew with bay leaf, onion, basil, oregano, bitters.

Potatoes, White. Mash, add freshly grated onion and nutmeg or chives and margarine.

Potatoes, Sweet. Cinnamon, nutmeg; mash with unsweetened orange juice, escallop with apples.

Cooked Cereal. Serve with fresh fruits.

CONDIMENTS

ALLOWED

allspice
almond extract
aniseed
basil
bay leaves
calcium sucaryl
caraway seeds
cardamom
carob
chili powder
chives
cinnamon
cocoa
curry powder
dill
garlic

ginger
horseradish root
juniper
lemon juice
mace
marjoram
mint
mustard, dry
nutmeg
onion juice, fresh
oregano
paprika
parsley
pepper (black, red, and white)
peppermint

pimiento
poppy seeds
poultry seasoning
purslane
rosemary
saccharin
saffron
sage
savory
sesame seeds
sorrel
tarragon
thyme
turmeric
vanilla extract
vinegar

LOW-SODIUM ANTACIDS:
Maalox, Di-Gel, Rolaids, Riopan, Wingel

AVOID

baking powder	pickles
baking soda	popcorn, salted
bouillon cubes	potato chips
catsup	pretzels
celery salt	relishes (commercial)
garlic salt	self-rising flour
horseradish, prepared	soups, canned
meat extracts	table salt
meat sauces	Worcestershire sauce
monosodium glutamate	Certain stomach antacids, laxatives, and
mustard, prepared	sedatives which contain sodium—take
onion salt	only what your doctor has prescribed.
oyster sauce	(Alka-Seltzer, Bromo Seltzer and Bi-SoDol are high in sodium.)

Below are foods that are allowed and not allowed on a low-cholesterol, low-saturated-fat, 4-gram sodium, and low-refined-carbohydrate diet.

WHAT TO EAT AND WHAT NOT TO EAT

FOOD GROUPS	ALLOWED	AVOID
MILK	Any milk containing 1 percent fat or less. Skim milk, nonfat milk, evaporated skim milk, buttermilk made from skim milk, drinks made from skim milk and cocoa powder. Nonfat dry milk powder. Yogurt made from skim milk.	Whole, low-fat, or 2 percent milk (latter allowed only on approval); drinks made with whole or low-fat milk; sweetened condensed milk; buttermilk made with whole or low-fat milk; milk drinks made with chocolate; imitation milk or nondairy creamers made with saturated fat.

	ALLOWED	**AVOID**
		Sweet cream, sour cream, half and half, whipping cream.
		Yogurt made with whole or low-fat milk (latter allowed on approval).
EGGS	Limit to three egg yolks per week including any used in cooking or food processing. Egg whites and cholesterol-free egg substitutes may be used as desired.	Egg yolks in excess of three per week.
CHEESE	Limit 2 cups low-fat cottage cheese per week.	*All processed cheese;* cream cheese; regular, low-fat, or salt-free cheese in excess of amounts allowed.
	Limit to 3 ounces per week any cheese with fat content of 45 percent or more. This includes Cheddar, brick, blue, Camembert, Edam, Gouda, Gruyère, Liederkranz, Limburger, Roquefort, or Swiss. *However, instead of this, you may have up to 4 ounces per week* of the following cheeses:* cheeses with fat content of 20–45 percent: mozzarella, ricotta, Parmesan, Jarlsberg, Romano, Norvegia, etc. (Part-	

*NOTE: You may substitute 4 ounces of a turkey-based meat product, e.g., ham or bologna, for your 4 ounces of cheese.

ALLOWED	AVOID
skim milk cheese still contains some whole milk or milk fat along with some skim milk.) Cheeses with fat content less than 20 percent are permitted more frequently: farmer cheese, baker's cheese, hoop cheese, and sapsago.	

**MEAT
FISH
POULTRY**

Meats are divided into two groups: Group I — high in cholesterol and saturated fat. Serving size — 3 ounces (weight after cooking with bones removed), 5 days per week (or a total of 15 ounces per week). Group II — lower in cholesterol and saturated fat. Serving size — no more than 6–8 ounces per day, 7 days per week. Meat (protein) substitutes are also listed with their serving sizes.

GROUP I (Red Meats) 15 ounces or 5 days per week only

ALLOWED	AVOID
Lean, well-trimmed beef including extra-lean roasts, ground beef, and baby beef. Lean, well-trimmed pork or Canadian bacon.* Lean, well-trimmed lamb, venison, or rabbit.	Organ meats including liver, kidney, heart, and sweetbreads. (Once or twice a month two ounces may be substituted for one egg.) Fatty or heavily marbled meats such as regular ground beef or hamburger, bacon, sausage, ham hocks, ham, spareribs, short ribs, corned beef, mutton, or cured meats.

*Canadian bacon limited to 4 ounces weekly.

ALLOWED	*AVOID*
MEAT FISH POULTRY	

ALLOWED	*AVOID*
Protein substitutes:	Luncheon meats such as bologna, salami, or other cold cuts and frankfurters.
Regular, creamed cottage cheese (1/4 cup = 1 ounce meat).	Commercially fried meat unless prepared in polyunsaturated oil.
Shrimp, sardines, and crab are limited to 3 ounces weekly.	Any meat prepared with sauces or gravies unless made with allowed ingredients. Canned meat products. Kosher meat.
	Packaged or frozen "convenience foods" unless made with allowed ingredients.★
GROUP II Veal	
Poultry including chicken, stewing hens, cornish hens, turkey, wild game birds such as duck, goose, or squab without skin or fat.	Poultry skin; domesticated duck or goose.
Turkey-based bologna, salami, pastrami, ham, or frankfurters. (Limit 4 ounces per week in place of cheese allowance.)	

★Try to select items in which sodium or salt is listed at the end of the label.

ALLOWED	*AVOID*
MEAT FISH POULTRY	
Protein substitutes:	Anchovies, fish roe, or caviar; commercially fried fish unless pre-
Fish including abalone, bass, catfish, crappie,	

	ALLOWED	*AVOID*
	cod, flounder, haddock, halibut, perch, pike, salmon, tuna, trout, turbot, etc. Fish canned in water. Clams, lobster, oysters, scallops, and eel. Textured vegetable protein (TVP) and meat extenders. Tofu.	pared in polyunsaturated oil; tuna or other fish canned in a saturated oil or vegetable broth.
	Dried beans, peas, or legumes without saturated fat or salt added; vegetarian baked beans.*	Any dried beans, peas, or legumes cooked with pork, ham or other animal fat including most commercially canned or prepared refried beans.

*Serving size = 1/2 cup

MEAT FISH POULTRY	Old - fashioned - style peanut butter (limit 1–2 tablespoons daily). Most unsalted, dry roasted or in-the-shell nuts including almonds, black or English walnuts, filberts, hickory nuts, peanuts, pecans, pine nuts, pistachios, hazelnuts, pinon and sunflower seeds. (Nuts are very high in fat and calories. Use in moderation if overweight.)	Regular peanut butter, i.e., peanut butter with hydrogenated fat added. Macadamia, cashew, and brazil nuts; salted nuts or any nuts roasted in saturated fat.
POTATOES RICE PASTA	White and sweet potatoes, yams, rice, macaroni, noodles, spaghetti, and other pastas prepared without eggs.	Commercially fried potatoes; salted snack chips such as potato or corn chips made with saturated fat.

	ALLOWED	AVOID
	Occasionally you may have unsalted corn or potato chips made with allowed oils.	Potato, rice, or pasta dishes with cheese or cream sauces unless made with allowed ingredients. Egg noodles.
BREADS	Any whole wheat, whole grain, or enriched bread. Bagels (except egg and salt), English muffins, pita bread, unsalted crackers, unsalted matzos, unsalted pretzels (made without fat), graham crackers, Melba toast, bread sticks, hamburger/hot dog buns, or other baked goods containing allowed ingredients. Corn tortillas or flour tortillas made with allowed oils. Flour, cornstarch, and cornmeal. Unsalted popcorn made with either no fat or polyunsaturated oil.	Egg or cheese breads, butter rolls, cheese crackers; bread, crackers, or rolls with salt toppings; commercially made French toast, sweet rolls, cinnamon rolls, Danish pastries, fruit or nut breads, or any baked product made with ingredients not allowed. Commercial mixes containing eggs, whole milk and saturated or hydrogenated fat for biscuits, cornbread, muffins, pancakes, waffles, bread, rolls, and bread stuffings.
	Most cooked, ready-to-eat and natural grain cereals except those containing coconut or saturated fat.	Any cereal containing coconut, coconut oil, or other ingredients not allowed. (Many granola cereals contain coconut; check the labels.)
VEGETA-BLES	Any fresh, frozen, or canned vegetables without saturated fat. Salt-free vegetable juices,	Vegetables prepared in salt brine, e.g., pickles, olives, and sauerkraut. Regular vegetable juice

ALLOWED	AVOID
e.g., low sodium V-8 juice (1/2 cup of regular vegetable juice is permitted daily). Most tomato products including tomato sauce, hot sauce, and enchilada sauce.	in excess of the amount allowed. Any buttered, creamed, or fried vegetables unless prepared with allowed ingredients. Vegetables commercially prepared with a cream sauce or butter.

FRUIT

ALLOWED	AVOID
Any fresh, dried, canned, or frozen fruit or fruit juice that does not have sugar or syrup added. Avocados are permitted in moderation.	Coconut. Canned fruit in light or heavy syrup.

FATS

ALLOWED	AVOID
Any polyunsaturated, liquid vegetable oil. Polyunsaturated soft tub margarines made from allowed oils.	THESE ARE SATURATED FAT PRODUCTS: butter, lard, shortening, suet, hydrogenated or hardened vegetable oil, and products containing these. Bacon, salt pork, or meat drippings containing fat. Cream sauces and gravies unless made with allowed ingredients. Sweet, sour, or whipped cream. Most nondairy creamers, whipped toppings, cream cheese, and sour cream substitutes.
Oil-based salad dressing such as French, Italian, or Russian (Limit 1 tablespoon daily).	
Mayonnaise made with allowed oil and containing a minimum of cholesterol.	
Homemade sour cream.	
It is best to limit the total amount of fat you consume to no more than 1–2 servings per day.	Salad dressing containing cheese, such as blue or Roquefort, unless counted as part of regular cheese allowance.
1 serving = Margarine .... 1 t. Salad Dressing ... 1 T. Mayonnaise ..... 1 t.	Coconut, palm, or palm kernel oil.

	ALLOWED	**AVOID**
	Oils .... 1 t. Almonds ..... 6 small Peanuts ....12 Tartar Sauce ..... 1 T. Sesame Seeds .... 1 T. Sunflower Seeds ....1-1/2 T. Reduced-calorie Mayonnaise ... 1 T. Diet Margarine .. 1 T.	Commercial garlic spread. Margarines which contain large amounts of saturated fat.
SOUPS	Unsalted clear broth, bouillon, or consomme without fat; any home-made cream or broth-based soup made from allowed ingredients.	Regular canned broth, bouillon and con-somme; packaged de-hydrated soups; any homemade or com-mercial soup made with ingredients not al-lowed. NOTE: Com-mercial soups are very high in salt; check with a dietitian for approval.
DESSERTS	Angel food cake, carob powder, gelatin, gra-ham crackers, sherbet, fruit juice ice; pudding, pie crusts, fruit pies, or any other dessert made with allowed ingredi-ents.	Any dessert made with ingredients not al-lowed. Most commer-cial cakes, pies, and cookies and mixes for same. Ice cream, ice milk. Fruit or cream pies and buttercream (bak-ery type) frostings. Pie crusts made with lard, shortening, or butter.
SWEETS	If you have elevated triglycerides and/or are overweight, avoid the following foods (other-wise use them spar-ingly): sugar, honey,	Chocolate and all candy not listed as allowed.

	ALLOWED	_AVOID_
	jam, jelly, marmalade, molasses, preserves, syrup. Pure sugar candies including hard candy, gum drops, jelly beans, marshmallows, plain mints, popsicles, regular gelatin dessert, sherbet, cake.	
BEVER-AGES	Coffee, decaffeinated coffee, tea, cereal beverages, and alcoholic beverages. NOTE: Limit alcohol intake to 1 drink per day if you are overweight or have elevated triglycerides. One drink = 12 ounces light beer, 3–4 ounces wine, or 1-1/2 ounces alcohol.	Softened water. Alcoholic beverages containing whole milk, cream, or coconut.
	Limit diet soda to 2 cans daily. (Diet Pepsi and Diet Rite Cola may be used more frequently.)	Regular soda and sweetened soft drinks.
CONDI-MENTS	Unsalted herbs and spices (i.e., garlic powder, not garlic salt); artificial flavorings and extracts. Catsup (1 tablespoon daily), soy sauce, vinegar, cocoa powder, carob powder. Cream sauces and gravies made with allowed ingredients. Weight Watcher TV dinners.	TV dinners other than those listed as allowed. Salt or seasonings in excess of 1/2 teaspoon per day. Bottled meat sauces, meat tenderizers, pickles, olives, mustard, and MSG (Accent). "Lite" salt or salt substitutes (allowed only if approved by physician).

10

The Exercise Factor

The human body—your body—was meant to move. To walk, bend, stretch, run, twist. Comfortably and easily. An inactive life, one that deprives your body of getting an adequate dosage of physical activity on a regular, systematic basis, could be lethal. In this chapter we will consider how your body *needs* activity to maintain even a modicum of fitness, and *demands* enlivened activity to achieve a level of health and well-being that will support a strong, vigorous life. You have seen on the Heart Test that inactivity is a risk factor in heart disease. It is a risk factor in other illnesses as well. People who lead inactive, sedentary lives run a higher risk of heart disease than those who engage in a regular exercise routine.

Here are some of the questions our patients frequently ask us when we prescribe a program of intensive exercise for them.

Is it true that exercise will change my outlook on life?

It can. For many people it builds self-confidence in their ability to manage their own lives. One of the most discouraging characteristics that I have witnessed among heart victims is their utter sense of having lost control over their own existence. They live in constant fear that they may suffer another heart attack and that this next one will be fatal, or that they will eventually end up with the same heart or brain condition that killed Dad or Mom. It is truly amazing how the small amount of control over their bodies that comes from even modest goals in an exercise program can dispel these fears. Control of even one part of your life can dilute the worry of life in so many ways. The faithful exerciser experiences a new life, a new vision, actually a more positive image of himself or herself by being able to achieve the goals that are set in regulated exercise programs. Vigorous physical accomplishments such as running five miles, swimming ten laps, hiking up a nearby mountain, are permanent reminders, even after the exercise period, that an active life is a healthy life, a life that is under your own control.

A short time ago I participated in a program in Florida with Dr. Kenneth Cooper, the father of aerobic exercise. (See page 193 for a definition of *aerobic*.) I slipped into the rear of the auditorium to hear one of the most articulate and inspiring lectures on exercise that I think I have ever heard. At the conclusion, he asked the packed audience, "And why do we exercise on a regular basis?" "Because it makes us feel so good!" was the spontaneous response.

If you begin an exercise program today, I can assure you that not only will you be a healthier person six months from now, but you will feel better, enjoy your life more, and have a more positive attitude about yourself, your limitations, and your capabilities. You will exercise your outlook on life as well as your body. When you pit yourself against a program that you create yourself, with some professional advice to keep you on the right track, you will reap unexpected rewards in the days to come. A sound exercise program could also help guarantee that there *will* be rewarding days to come.

Is it possible to fool myself into thinking I am physically fit?

Yes, *physical fitness* is one of those slippery terms that the average person finds hard to pin down and define accurately. When you listen to people talk about being fit, it is sometimes astounding to hear what they think constitutes fitness. Many people who took the Heart Test, for instance, were shocked to discover that their risk for heart disease was higher than they supposed. They concluded rightly that they were not as physically fit as they thought they were. Yet, prior to the Heart Test, there were no clues, no indications that they were living at substandard levels of physical fitness, particularly cardiovascular fitness. It is easy to fool ourselves into thinking we are fit.

One person plays a round of golf on Saturday, eighteen holes even, and believes that this keeps him fit. A woman climbs three flights of stairs at work each day, rather than take the elevator, because she read somewhere that we must build these little exercise rituals into our average day, and so she assumes that this alone maintains her fitness. Some people conclude that they are in good physical shape if they have not been seriously sick in a year or two, as if the absence of illness is what defines health and fitness. Certainly, all these are indicators of a person's overall fitness but they are only indicators. They themselves are not what makes a person fit, and certainly not in terms of cardiovascular fitness. In some ways they are like the person who spent all afternoon horseback riding and returned home feeling hale and hearty, feeling in great shape. Actually it was the horse that was in great shape!

Should I see a doctor first?

Many people wonder whether it is safe to begin an intensive exercise program without first consulting their doctor for a general physical examination. You already have some indication of the answer to this question. What was your *total* score on the Heart Test? If it was above 19, you should consult your doctor before beginning *any* exercise program. If your score was below 19 and you are under thirty-five years of age and are in generally good health, a program that follows the guidelines given in the next section of this chapter can be initiated without a doctor's approval. There are certain conditions, though, that warrant a medical screening before you begin.

See your doctor if:

1. you are over thirty-five and have not been aerobically active;
2. you are at a high risk for coronary artery disease, that is, you have two or more of the major risk factors of family history, high blood pressure, elevated cholesterol, cigarette smoking, diabetes;

3. you have recently recuperated from a serious illness, such as hepatitis, and/or are still on medication or restricted diet;
4. you find you cannot keep up with people your own age and sex in normal activities and recreations. You should be able to compete with someone of your own age and sex and not feel greatly disadvantaged. An early sign of heart disease is fatigue, especially fatigue measured against yourself. In other words, if you could climb to the top of the hill in February and you find you can't make it come May, something is wrong.

Note: A Heart Test score of 40 or more DEMANDS THAT YOU SEE YOUR PHYSICIAN.

What are the components of fitness?

First, we should say that a good definition of fitness ought to aim at your own personal capabilities. It should challenge you to achieve and maintain the capability of living, working, and playing at your optimal level of efficiency. Whatever your optimal level of efficiency is, it requires your heart, blood vessels, lungs, and muscles to function at their most efficient capabilities. Remember that what is most efficient for you may not be the same for your friends or neighbors. You know the standard of active living you want to enjoy. For this, you need to be fit. You will need *endurance, strength,* and *flexibility*—the three components of physical fitness. Of these, endurance is the most important for our purposes because it is the most accurate indicator of cardiovascular fitness.

Endurance is your ability to produce energy over a long period of time. Energy is burned up like fuel in a car. If you are able to produce the energy you need to achieve the active goals you set for yourself for the length of time you wish to engage in them, then you have endurance.

Strength is the maximum amount of force that a muscle can generate. When your muscles give out from too much exertion, you know you have reached the limit of your strength. With practice your muscles grow stronger and are able to generate more force.

Flexibility is the range of motion through which a joint can move. It involves joints, ligaments, tendons, and muscles. Being flexible decreases your risk of injury and improves your coordination and agility.

All of these fitness components are some indication of age. As you grow older you usually decline in strength, flexibility, and endurance. By engaging in steady exercise over the years you can retard or delay these signs of aging. Staying active is a way of staying youthful and retaining your vitality and warding off the degenerative symptoms of old age.

Sometimes when we run a fitness profile on people at the Heart Institute, we find that their fitness and their biological age do not match up. For example, a thirty-seven-year-old woman may have the fitness profile of a fifty-year-old-woman. The reverse holds, too. Some older people have the fitness profile of someone much younger than they are.

If this is true, should I ever be satisfied with my level of fitness?

Of course, you may be satisfied with your level of fitness once you have achieved the level you need. We should be satisfied with worthy accomplishments. But since you know that the components of physical fitness will decline over the years, thus forcing you into a less active mode of living, you should not be satisfied to the point that you are willing to give up an active life-style and retire to the rocker on the porch when you don't really have to. You may have a career that demands long hours and fatiguing responsiblities, or a family life that is enthusiastic and all-consuming, or a favorite weekend sport that demands physical energy while offering you sociability and competitive release of pent-up tensions. All of these are worthy activities that you should want to enjoy as long as possible. Only you know the physical, mental, and emotional requirements that will keep you totally fit to meet the excitement of your entire life with vigor and enthusiasm. This, then, is the measure of fitness that you should be concerned about. By changing your definition of fitness to mean the optimal end of your capabilities— rather than the middle, which would mean "just getting by"—you have a challenge, a standard of fitness that will motivate you to never be satisfied with a level that does not allow *you* to do what you want to do to the best of your ability. By considering fitness to be a future goal, constantly luring you farther along, rather than a static condition of your present life, you will become fit—and stay fit—in your efforts to achieve it.

Why can't I just be average? Isn't it good to be average?

When someone who hasn't exercised in years asks me if he or she is fit, I'm tempted to tell them to assume the worst, that whatever their current level of fitness is and no matter how they seem to be average as compared to their friends, they should not be satisfied with it. Why such a pessimistic answer? Basically, I think we are justified in *underestimating* our general health because we live in a society that deprives us of so many of the basic conditions for optimum sound health and energetic living. Ironically, modern American society is "too easy" to live in. That's right, too easy! Consequently, it is also easy to *die* in. We've finally achieved what every generation before us was striving for, an easier life, and now that we've done it, we find that it's also hard—hard to keep from having that fatal heart attack or stroke. What an irony, that it is hard to stay healthy to enjoy a life that is so easy! It is also increasingly difficult to get the clean air, the nutritious meals, and the rest and relaxation that are also components in human health.

Should we blame heart disease on technology?

Yes and no. Technology has taken a lot of the physical strain out of life and so we exert less and less physical energy to accomplish the same tasks on which our fathers and mothers expended considerable muscle power, and, in the process, kept themselves fit. Even that round of golf on the weekend is easier with a motorized golf cart! I admit that few, if any, of us would prefer to return to those so-called good old days and have to sacrifice the modern conveniences that would very quickly turn them into "bad old days" for us. Nevertheless, the trend in the last generation has been to replace as much physical labor as possible with mechanized and motor-powered technology, and in other ways to reduce the amount of physical exertion that is needed for our high standard of living. It seems that we can't win. Every time we make life easier, we make it harder—to stay fit.

Heart attacks have become a major cause of death only in the twentieth century. Coincidentally, this parallels the very years when more and more people began using automobiles for transportation, between 1930 and 1960. Of course, there are more reasons for this upsurge in heart disease than four-wheel drive and power steering! But the analogy and the lesson contained in it are worth remembering. As our modern way of living grows physically less strenuous, so, too, in its own way, does your heart become less able to withstand even the normal strains and stresses to which it is subject.

Teddy Roosevelt, a keen sportsman and exercise enthusiast, encouraged Americans in his day, before the automobile invaded our land, to lead what he called the "strenuous life." In his own way, he challenged Americans not to remain at an average level of fitness. He didn't mean that everyone should hunt lions on African safaris like he did, and organize private armies to storm up San Juan Hill, or even that everyone had to carry a bit stick. What he advocated was an intense enthusiasm and tough commitment to whatever activity you were engaged in even if it be collecting stamps or butterflies. He did promote physical exercise, both indoor and outdoor, to replace that hardy frontier life-style that was fast disappearing at the turn of the century.

I've never considered myself strenuous. What can I do?

Don't let the word *strenuous* scare you off! It is a relative term that applies to *your* current condition. It is a *progressive* concept that can keep pace with you now and in the years to come, so that even at an advanced old age, you can enjoy good health and bodily strength to continue to live at your maxmimum potential. You are living at the end of the twentieth century and are witnessing the depressing results of the wonders of our modern age—a generation of Americans who grow more susceptible to cardiovascular ailments as they grow lazier in their physical activities. It does take a commitment to a vigorous or a strenuous life to stay physically fit in modern America.

Why is everyone pushing aerobic exercise? What does aerobic mean?

Aerobic means "with oxygen." Aerobic exercises provide your body with large amounts of oxygen needed to energize the sustained, rhythmical movements that comprise the exercise. In the process, aerobics guarantee optimum cardiovascular functioning. Most aerobic exercises are the natural movements of human life—walking, running, swimming, jumping—stepped up to a higher level of energy. This in turn accelerates the cardiorespiratory process to a quicker and more efficient level. For the most part, aerobic activities are rhythmic, as are most movements and cycles in Nature. When you engage in aerobic exercises you feel vigorous and in tune with the rhythmic order. Aerobic movements are Nature's way of providing you with all the cardiovascular benefits we have just considered: increased pumping efficiency, better oxygen utilization, a lower resting heart rate, and, in some cases, lower blood pressure.

Aerobic exercises work on large muscle groups for extended periods of time. No other mode of exercise involves these large muscles or keeps them continuously active for a proper length of time. Because large muscles have more cells and because during the exercise period there is an increased demand for energy, your heart is forced to pump large supplies of blood to these muscle areas in your body. So you can see that aerobic exercises activate the heart, lungs, and blood vessel system as well as muscles. No other exercises are quite as complete.

But I like to do push-ups, and on Saturdays I play right field on a softball team. Aren't these good enough?

They aren't the same at all as aerobic exercise. These are *anaerobic* exercises, literally "without oxygen." Exercises that fall into this category, like calisthenics and most team sports, produce energy for body movements, but it is energy that does not require extra amounts of oxygen over a sustained period of time. That is why they are called anaerobic—without oxygen. When you think about most calisthenics and team sports activities, you will realize that they do not ask you to move large muscle groups for an extended period of time, say, thirty to forty minutes, nonstop. They require short bursts of movement followed by time to rest or slow down. These patterns of exercise movements do not demand the same volume of oxygen as aerobics and consequently do not demand the heart, lungs, and blood vessel system to work as hard. With these your heart and respiratory system do not get an extended training session and they do not derive the benefits that we have seen are so important for health. In short, it is not possible to keep your cardiovascular system fit by anaerobic exercises. You may notice that some calisthenics and sports activities, like push-ups and bowling, do raise your heart rate but it is not to the same degree as aerobics, nor for the same amount of time, and not by the same mechanism, that is, the need for increased oxygen transport. In summary, exercises that are not genuinely and continuously aerobic in nature do not allow your heart to beat at a conditioning rate for a long enough time to bring you the cardiovascular benefits you need.

Why are aerobics so good for losing weight?

Aerobics are the best type of exercise for weight control, although very little weight can be lost without the proper low-calorie diet to supplement the exercise program. You may, however, see changes in your body composition after several months of training. What you are noticing is the loss of *fat* weight and an increase in *lean* body weight. Not only will you feel better, but you'll begin to look better, too. The muscles you use will begin to firm up and the weight you lose will be distributed over your entire body. This is the only proper way to reduce. You may have seen various gimmick exercises or even mechanical exercisers that promise you weight loss on selected parts of your body, such as your waist or thighs or hips. These "slimnastics" programs mislead gullible people into thinking that "spot-reduction" techniques will take weight off any part of the body they desire. Unfortunately, this is not so. Weight loss is uniform over the whole body and occurs only from vigorous rhythmic movements that are frequent and sustained. In other words, the human body loses weight from aerobic activities.

In addition, many people who are faithful aerobic exercisers notice a decrease in their appetites. This is especially true during the hour or so immediately after the exercise session. They simply don't get hungry for a while. They aren't in the mood to eat large meals. Part of the reason for this is that there are changes in your metabolism from exercising that may kill your appetite. By scheduling your exercise period right before a mealtime, you can forestall your hunger and maybe even get by on eating less.

Will exercise actually strengthen my heart?

It depends on what you mean by "strengthen." It is not exactly the same kind of strengthening that occurs when you exercise your biceps or triceps. You do not use the same method of exercise, either. Nevertheless, the heart is a muscle and like other muscles it requires a workout to achieve and maintain its optimal strength. Here's what happens when you exercise your heart by aerobic methods.

You will have greater pumping efficiency. This means that your heart will be able to perform the same amount of work with less effort. Now, the work your heart performs is to pump blood through the yards and yards of blood vessels throughout your body. With exercise, you can increase its stroke volume, the amount of blood pumped out with each contraction. If your heart can send out the same amount of blood with fewer contractions, it is more energy efficient. It is more economical, similar to your car when it is idling. The motor continues to run, the engine processes gasoline, but with much less strain.

Furthermore, with systematic exercise, your heart will have a faster recovery rate. The recovery rate is the amount of time it takes for your heartbeat to return from the elevated level it was exercising at to its normal resting rate. You may have seen people who are not in shape huff and puff and sweat for a long time after physical activity while their hearts continue to pound away as if they were still engaged in the activity. This is obviously a misuse of energy for a heart to work harder than it needs to. But with exercise, your heart will return to its resting rate more quickly. With regular exercise, your resting heart rate itself may become lower. Again, the same principle is involved. Your heart can perform its function more economically and more efficiently with less energy.

So in this sense, a trained heart, like other trained muscles, performs better. It has more strength and endurance. It is conditioned or trained and consequently can beat more effectively and beautifully than untrained hearts.

Is it good for heart patients to exercise?

Yes, they, too, can increase their heart's efficiency by faithfully exercising. Naturally, they must be put on a carefully monitored program and progress gradually. But exercise is a perfect remedy for postoperative patients. What we hope to do with heart patients is to increase collateral circulation to the heart through exercise. The part of the heart that suffers ischemia (a condition in which the tissue does not receive enough blood) will be supplied by alternate vascular routes that aerobic exercise produces. This collateral circulation tends to develop when more demand for oxygen is placed on the muscle. Aerobic exercises create this demand for more oxygen and so the heart victim acquires extra vessels to supply the heart with blood.

Won't exercise tire me out?

Of course; after exercising you may be exhausted. You should be—for a while at least. But over the course of the day you will find what many of our patients discover, that your overall energy level is higher. You will be able to exert yourself in other tasks with less strain than a person who is not in shape. We say that topnotch athletes perform almost as if they weren't trying or as if it were a tremendously easy feat. And yet we know it is not. We know they try hard. It's just that the visible signs of strain and exertion are not always there. Good athletes can expend enormous energy gracefully. Why? Partly because their hearts are conditioned to supply the muscles of the body with blood and oxygen more efficiently. Consequently, their bodies do not tire as easily. In addition, the delivery of oxygen directly to the millions of cellular destinations throughout the body is accomplished more efficiently with an aerobically trained heart because the process of extracting oxygen from the blood is more efficient. What all this means is that exercise will not wear you out in the long run. The immediate exhaustion you may feel after your workout session quickly leaves and when it does it leaves you with the feeling that you have more energy than you had before.

Is it true that if I exercise I won't get sick?

No. But we have noticed that committed exercisers are less prone to illness, and when they do occasionally get sick, they don't let it debilitate them as much as do people who do not get regular exercise. One reason for this is that people who exercise are more health conscious than others. Their minds are more attuned to what is good for them physically. They are also more reluctant to let a cold or headache wipe them out for the entire day. In some sense they have more stamina and make it through the year with fewer days lost to recuperating in bed. In general, even though there are no hard clinical data yet to explain this, it is our observation at the Institute that exercise leads to more productive living all around. At least our patients tell us so, and we can see it in their lives. For example, it seems that exercisers can cope with stress better. Perhaps this is because they must manage their time more efficiently in order to get in their accustomed exercise sessions. We know that better time management is one way to reduce stress. Exercise is also a natural way to blow off steam. It helps us unwind and get rid of the tension and anxiety that are associated with stress.

In terms of cardiovascular illness, exercise also affects blood values. Your cholesterol level should be lower when you exercise and some studies have indicated that HDLs increase with exercise. You will lose weight by burning up calories. Physical activity of the aerobic type is known to lower one's blood pressure. So in terms of several risk factors in heart disease, exercise is one way to lower them. Knowing you are taking practical steps to reduce your chances of heart attacks and strokes is also good for your self-confidence, for knowing that you have taken charge of your life and are in control. A psychic result that many exercisers report is this sense of well-being and self-confidence that comes from knowing that they can jog that extra mile or swim those additional laps across the pool. There's no getting around it, sustained and rhythmical exercise is Nature's way of keeping human beings fit.

What do you prescribe for a home exercise program?

No matter what type of aerobic exercise you decide to do, there are four key components that should be part of any exercise prescription. These are mode, duration, frequency, and intensity. Let's consider these individually and determine how each figures into a home program.

Mode

Mode means the type of exercise or the form that your exercising takes, like hiking, swimming, running, and so on. It should be some type of aerobic exercise as opposed to isometrics, calisthenics, or recreational team sports. The most common aerobic exercises that people can do on their own include walking, biking, swimming, jogging, and hiking. An aerobic mode of exercise is preferred because of the cardiovascular benefits that can be derived from it. Recreational sports and the "start and stop" type of exercises, like calisthenics, may improve your flexibility, muscular endurance, and strength, but they do not exercise the cardiorespiratory system to the same extent. Since we are primarily concerned with cardiovascular fitness to reduce our risk factors, only an aerobic activity gets our full endorsement as your primary mode of exercise.

Duration

Duration means how long you exercise each session. We believe that a minimum of twenty minutes is absolutely essential. Continuous movement for as much as thirty to sixty minutes, however, is optimal. You should remember that duration and intensity (see below) are interrelated. On some days you may not feel up to running or swimming as long as you usually do, or you may not have time for it. On these occasions you can increase your intensity and exercise for a shorter period of time without losing cardiovascular benefits. This is important especially for heart patients who cannot exercise at high intensity. They can derive aerobic benefits by exercising a little longer but at a lower intensity.

Frequency

Frequency is the number of sessions per week you exercise. Three to five sessions weekly are necessary for optimal improvement and weight loss. Exercising every day of the week is not advised because it can lead to overfatigue and musculoskeletal injuries. If you exercise the bare minimum of three times a week, make sure you work out on nonconsecutive days so that you stretch your exercise time over the entire week and allow rest-up days in between. Increasing from three to five times a week will increase the benefits, but beyond five times, the benefits do not seem to outweigh the incidence of injury and fatigue.

Intensity

Intensity is the most important component in your exercise prescription. It is defined as "how hard" or "how strenuously" you exercise. How do you know? The best way to calculate your intensity is by clocking your heart rate while or after you exercise to see how much demand was placed upon your heart. In other words, how hard did it work? How fast did it beat beyond what it normally does when you rest? (Everyone has a resting heart rate, the number of beats per minute while at rest.)

The range for resting heartbeats is sixty to eighty beats per minute. Some people have an inherently low resting heart rate. Don't be confused by assuming that if *yours* is low you have the cardiovascular fitness of someone engaged in aerobic training. The fact that aerobics may lower your resting heart rate applies as a benefit only to someone who does aerobics! If you lead a sedentary life-style and never exercise, you are not better off because your resting heart rate is low. Someone else who does exercise is getting more cardiovascular benefits even if his or her resting heart rate is higher than yours. This is because they have been exercising at their target heart rates.

What Is a Target Heart Rate?

The intensity with which you exercise should gradually increase to a specified target that we call your target heart rate. Your target heart rate should be in a range of 70 percent to 85 percent of your maximum heart rate. Here is how to calculate your target heart rate:

Fill in the blanks to calculate your target heart rate.
Subtract your age, _____ , from 220 = _____ maximum heart rate.
Multiply maximum heart rate, _____ , first by .7 and then by .85 = _____ and _____ range of target heart rate.

For example, if you are thirty-six years old, your maximum heart rate would be 220 minus 36, or 184. Now 184, your maximum heart rate, multiplied by .7 and .85 equals 128 and 156. This range, 128 to 156, is the number of heartbeats (or pulse beats) per minute that assures an exercise intensity to provide the optimum in cardiovascular benefits. At a heart rate of 128 you would be working at the low end of the range, whereas a rate of 156 would be toward the upper end of the scale. A lower intensity is appropriate for the person beginning an exercise program. Conditioned people are able to comfortably train at a higher percentage of their aerobic capacity.

Since you will probacly not want to clock your pulse beat for an entire minute after you exercise, and because your beat begins to return to your normal resting rate very quickly when you stop working out anyway, divide your target heart rate by 6 to get the number of beats for ten seconds. In this case, 23–27 beats for ten seconds would indicate the target heart rate was achieved.

Let's take a look at how aerobic exercises compare with other exercise in terms of intensity of your target heart rate. When you work out at 75 percent of your maximum heart rate for thirty minutes, your heart rate would look like this on a graph:

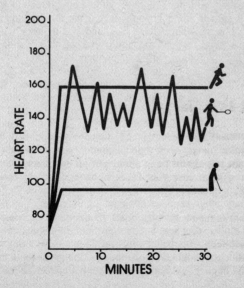

On the other hand, certain recreational sports, like softball, volleyball, basketball, and racket sports, with their "start and stop" rhythms do not let you reach your target heart rate and sustain it for the required amount of time. You may elevate your heart rate intermittently, but this is not the aerobic effect you are seeking. See graph for what your heart rate would look like while playing racketball.

Similarly, leisure-time activities, like golf or bowling, in which there is very little intensity, may increase your heart rate to some degree but certainly not to a maximum target rate. These produce very few cardiovascular benefits. See graph once again.

Besides providing cardiovascular benefits, what else does intensity promise?

The most crucial component in your exercise program, as you can now see, is intensity. You have to work hard for at least twenty minutes. It is best if you keep it up for thirty minutes to a full hour. At first you will have to stop and take your pulse to make sure you are exercising at your target heart rate. Some people feel embarrassed to do this in public, but there is really nothing wrong with it. Eventually after you exercise a lot your own body signals will tell you that you are at your target heart rate. You'll learn what it feels like, and you'll know when you are at it. A good test that you are overdoing it is if you cannot carry on a conversation with your partner. You'll know then that you are working out too strenuously. So slow down a bit.

You will also discover that maintaining a training level of intensity will, in the long run, make it more enjoyable for you to exercise. At first the extra energy that must be used by the muscles seems overwhelming. You may grow tired and think that your heart will never be able to supply enough oxygen to your muscles for the energy demands that your exercise is making. But the wonderful thing about aerobic intensity is that very soon you will increase your capacity to supply your body with that extra oxygen-rich blood. Exercising will then be more fun.

You may even become addicted to exercise. You'll enjoy feeling healthy and actually *want* to exercise. It takes time, though. Don't expect results overnight. But in about three weeks you should feel a lot better physically. In six weeks you'll be committed to exercise. Be sure, though, that you don't give it a mere one-week try, get sore and achy, give up, and say, "Well,

I tried it, and it's not for me.'' Give it a chance. Give your heart a chance to adjust to the ''strenuous life'' you have chosen for yourself. What quality of life or degree of activity do you really want for yourself? You should not settle for a low level of living simply because you are out of shape and find physical exertions to be too fatiguing. The human body was created to be active. Your body should crave action. You owe it to yourself, your body, and especially your heart, to let your life become as vitally active and energetic as possible. You'll feel better and probably live longer.

Is it safe to pick an exercise and plunge right in?

Only if it's swimming. Even then it is advised that you test the water before you plunge. You may be standing at the shallow end! Seriously, every exercise program should be *progressive*. It should begin easy and get progressively harder and more demanding. This is one of the most important aspects of exercise in order to guarantee your perseverance in it. Nothing is more discouraging than to initiate an exercise program that is too advanced only to find out you cannot perform well. It can also be detrimental to your health. Progressing sensibly from easy to hard will also guarantee you the optimal benefits to your cardiovascular system and prevent unnecessary injuries and fatigue. Here is the progression we suggest:

In intensity:

1. Spend the first three weeks in *preconditioning*. This means that you should gradually strengthen your legs, learn how to breathe deeply, and master the required movements of the exercise. Don't set yourself any goals these three weeks other than getting a good generalized understanding of what is involved in your chosen form of exercise. Gradually become accustomed to working at a higher heart rate than you are used to while resting.
2. During the next six weeks, shoot for a target heart rate that is about 70 percent of your maximum rate, no more. Stay at this pace for the entire six weeks, near the end of which you will realize the need to increase it.
3. After these six weeks, increase your target heart rate 5 to 10 percent so that you once again feel you are getting an adequate workout. Caution: Never exceed 85 percent of your maximum rate.

In duration:

1. In your first weeks, you should work out for three- to five-minute intervals interspersed with one-minute rest periods. This may seem slow to you, but it is best not to overdo it in these initial days.
2. As you become more confident and you notice the exercise is getting easier for you, increase the workout periods and decrease the rest periods.
3. Your goal is to reach twenty minutes of continuous exercise. Remember, though, that this is the minimum goal. It would be better if you could work out for thirty to sixty minutes.

In frequency:

1. Your first few weeks should find you exercising three nonconsecutive days each week. Don't exercise on consecutive days without time in between to let your muscles relax and respond to the training stimulus.
2. Increase to four days per week when you feel that you are ready. Later add a fifth day.
3. Do not exercise more than five days a week. Your chances of fatigue and consequent injuries do not justify the meager benefits that accrue with a sixth or seventh day of exercise. In other words, your body and your heart have reached a kind of saturation point at six days, after which the benefits of additional exercise are minimal.

Is warming up important, even on hot days?

Yes, just as cooling down is important on cold days. Every time you exercise you should incorporate the three main components of exercise. All professional athletes will attest to the necessity of these steps if you want to assure the greatest degree of safety and proper care of your body.

Here are the three phases of your daily exercise session.

1. **Warm up.** Spend about five to ten minutes stretching your muscles, bending at the waist, limbering your joints, and in general loosening yourself up so that you will not pull a muscle when you actually begin to exercise. In addition to

flexibility exercises, a complete warm-up also includes a modified level of the specific exercise or sport. Bat a tennis ball around a few times before you begin to play seriously. Walk briskly before you run.

2. **Work out.** This is your twenty- to sixty-minute period of continuous aerobic exercise.

3. **Cool down.** When you have finished exercising, spend a few minutes still moving, walking, bending, stretching to let your heart rate and breathing rate return to your normal level. Don't just immediately collapse into a chair and pop open a canned drink. Cool down gradually.

PROGRESSIVE CONDITIONING CHART

	WEEK		SUN.	MON.	TUE.	WED.	THUR.	FRI.	SAT.	Goals
Pre-Conditioning	1	HR								1. Become accustomed to working with higher than RHR.
		Duration								
	2	HR								2. Work out in 3- to 5-minute intervals with 1-minute rest period, gradually increasing work and decreasing rest, reaching 20 minutes continuous exercise.
		Duration								
	3	HR								
		Duration								
										3. Exercise 3 nonconsecutive days per week.
Conditioning	4	HR								1. Increase THR to 70 percent of MHR.
		Duration								
	5	HR								2. 30–60 minutes of continuous exercise.
		Duration								
	6	HR								
		Duration								3. Exercise 4–5 days per week.
	7	HR								
		Duration								
	8	HR								4. At end of 6 weeks increase THR 5–10 percent, never exceeding 85 percent MHR.
		Duration								
	9	HR								
		Duration								

Record HR (heart rate), minutes of continuous exercise, and number of days per week exercising.

Calculate THR and MHR.

220 − your age _____ = MHR

MHR × .7 = _____ } Range of THR
MHR × .85 = _____

Resting Heart Rate RHR:

Target Heart Rate THR:

Maximum Heart Rate MHR:

I've noticed that a lot of people who exercise wear brightly colored outfits and have partners. Is this really necessary?

Yes and no. There are things you must do to keep exercising from becoming boring. There are also things you will learn about safety. Special outfits and exercise partners can help in both areas.

Here are some other general guidelines to keep your exercise routine safe and fun.

General guidelines:

1. Dress comfortably. Some people think that if they wear extra clothing they will lose weight by sweating more profusely. The result, however, is the loss of water, not fat. Water does not contain calories, anyway, so there is no fat loss in water loss. Furthermore, excessive dehydration can lead to heat stroke. Guzzling water at the end of your exercise period will only put the water weight right back on. So wear loose-fitting outfits that give you room to move around in. Protect your head during cold temperatures in order to contain body heat. Most of the heat your body loses is from the top of your head. Wear layered clothing so you can conveniently peel off layers once you have warmed up. In hot weather, wear less clothing.

2. Wear protective shoes. The basic components of good shoes are that they give your feet maximum support, cushion the heels, and allow enough room for the toes to move around and spread a bit.

3. Plan to exercise prior to eating. This will cut down on your appetite, and allow you to exercise when your heart does not have to send extra blood to the stomach for food digestion. If you must exercise after a meal, wait one to two hours before you do.

4. On very hot days drink plenty of fluids before exercising to compensate for the water lost in sweat. Dehydration is dangerous.

5. Since most aerobic exercise can be done at any time of day, alter your routine when you can. Look for variety. Vary your time, your route, even your partner. Have fun.

6. Don't be afraid or hesitant to exercise when you are bone-tired and most lethargic. Exercise is a perfect way to revitalize your body and spirits.

7. Don't smoke. Smoking constricts the blood vessels and decreases the delivery of oxygen to the muscles. Smoking negates the benefits of regular endurance exercise. Only minimal endurance improvement will be made if you continue to smoke.

How can I decide which aerobic exercise is right for me?

People often have a hard time choosing what kind of exercise they should do. Many times the problem isn't just a failure to decide but a *failure to eliminate excuses* not to exercise at all. There are an infinite number of excuses the human mind can think up not to exercise. "It's too hot where I live." "I can't afford to build a swimming pool." "I've had a fear of bicycles since I was twelve." "I sweat too much." "I'm too busy with my career and my family." "I don't want to buy special shoes." And the list goes on and on. It's true that there may be certain exercises that are not right for you, but don't become a victim of "excusitis."

If we allowed excuses to rule our lives, we could all think up some reason not to exercise, especially if the exercise has any potential for injury. My friend and colleague Dr. Denton Cooley, the famous heart surgeon in Texas, is a good example of this. He has always been an active sportsman, no doubt to release the tension of a stressful occupation, as well as to indulge in his love of sport. I'm sure he has never particularly worried about an injury that might affect his career. Not long ago, however, he fractured his wrist on the tennis court. The injury did not stop him from operating—even in a cast—and now he's back to the sport again. If you are serious about modifying your risk factors for heart disease, your better self will not listen to flimsy excuses.

This section will help you decide rationally which aerobic exercise fits your present condition by evaluating the demands and requirements of each. We will look at the more popular aerobic activities and compare them in terms of what types of people can best participate in them, what precautions to take, what problems might arise, what types of equipment, if any, are needed, and what we at the Arizona Heart Institute recommend to you to make your exercise more enjoyable and beneficial.

Running

Running has become extremely popular in the last decade. Marathon races, fun runs, books on running, running clubs, and even running boutiques where you can buy the latest in running shoes and outfits have sprung up all over the country. Is running for you?

Participants. An average level of fitness is needed to begin running. It is not recommended for individuals with degenerative orthopedic problems, weak joints, or who are seriously overweight.

Recommendations. Running is the most efficient training method in terms of calories burned for the amount of time spent. In other words, it is extremely economical. You get maximum benefits back for the amount of time and energy you expend. You should run with someone of a comparable fitness level if you want to run with a partner. Someone whose pace is significantly slower or faster than your own can frustrate your progress.

Precautions. Running is known to increase the incidence of joint trauma. Let's face it, running is hard on the feet and lower extremities. The force on your feet is about three times your body weight. This does not mean that it is unnatural or dangerous for the average person. But if you have orthopedic problems or weak joints, you should not begin a running program without first consulting your doctor. Similarly, overweight people may come down on their feet too heavily. If you are extremely overweight, you should consider non-weight-bearing activities, like swimming or biking, either as preconditioning methods to reduce your weight so that you can eventually run or as alternative conditioning activities in themselves.

Walking

Walking is a universal activity that we underrate as exercise. Almost everyone does some walking every day. Systematic and conscious effort can turn walking into an aerobic activity that will give you the cardiorespiratory benefits of other forms of aerobics.

Participants. Anyone who can walk without orthopedic difficulties can turn walking into an aerobic activity.

Recommendations. Walking one mile at a brisk clip will burn off 100 calories. This is the same number of calories you would burn off if you ran one mile. Of course, by running you would consume these calories in less time. But whether you walk or run, one mile equals 100 calories.

Precautions. Make sure your feet are in good walking condition. If you have foot problems, consult a physician before you begin serious walking. You will need comfortable, flexible, well-fitting walking shoes. Problems that arise from walking are usually environmental: rough terrain, bad weather, and industrial or automotive pollutants that can irritate your respiratory system. The best walking is done at a time and place where there is a minimum of irritants.

Biking

Biking outdoors is an enjoyable aerobic activity because it provides the exhilaration of movement, travel, and novelty that more stationary exercises cannot offer. If you live in an area with frequent inclement temperatures or a neighborhood that does not have safe cycling routes, you can invest in a stationary bicycle to use in your home.

Participants. People of all ages and all levels of fitness can bike. It is an ideal sport for overweight individuals to reduce with because it does not require the heavy pounding of the total weight upon the feet and ankles. People with degenerative arthritis of the hip, however, will find it painful because of the tension that builds up in the hip due to resistance.

Recommendations. Biking compares with running on a 4:1 basis. Biking four miles is equivalent to running for one mile in terms of calories burned. Pedaling at a low resistance and a high frequency on a stationary bike can achieve the same cardiovascular results as pedaling at high resistance and low frequency if the heart rate is the same.

Precautions. Biking has a high injury rate. The same environmental hazards apply as to walking (see above). In addition, traffic can be menacing to your pace, causing you to stop and start according to traffic patterns and intersections. Traffic can also be dangerous to life and limb. Wear protective gear like a helmet, knee pads, elbow protectors, etc. The discomfort you may initially experience with the seat can be eliminated by proper adjustment or a custom seat. Always make sure your bicycle is well maintained, well oiled, clean, with sufficient air in the tires, and has good brakes. Reflectors and lights are a must for night riding. If you invest in a stationary bike, be aware that most people do not stay with them very long due to the boredom and the urge to ride outdoors.

Rope Jumping

Little girls and prizefighters—an unlikely combo! But jumping rope is not just for them anymore. More and more people have discovered the aerobic rewards in this simple activity that requires only a rope and a good pair of shoes. Recent studies, however, have shown that it is not the substitute for jogging that some people have purported it to be.

Participants. Again, this is not an exercise for the overweight and those with weak ankles or foot problems. Otherwise, rope jumping can be engaged in by people of all ages who are at a moderate fitness level. We do not recommend it for people with arthritis, bone problems, or poor balance.

Recommendations. Only 80 percent of the muscles are used in jumping compared with those used in running. Claims that ten minutes of jumping rope is equal to thirty minutes of jogging are unfounded in terms of physiological training. Equal amounts of genuine aerobic time jumping rope, however, will produce the same cardiovascular effect as if you were running. In other words, twenty minutes with the rope equals twenty minutes of running. Boredom is a factor to consider, too. Even spinning around doesn't change the scenery or the activity very significantly. Silly little jingles may help, but don't count on it.

Precautions. Jump on a soft surface or a carpet to alleviate impact trauma as much as possible. Be sure your shoes have sufficient padding under the toes and ball of your foot. If you find that your knees or joints hurt from too much jumping, you should either jump less or consult a podiatrist.

Lap Swimming

If you have year-round access to a large enough pool, you can make swimming laps your form of aerobic exercise. It takes, however, a little more effort to swim laps than what most people are accustomed to who associate swimming with summer and holiday recreation. Swimming for health is not leisure-time activity. It's work.

Participants. You must have a certain skill level to derive aerobic benefits from swimming. It takes a strong swimmer, like a Red Cross intermediate or beyond. It is, after all, more than just splashing around in the water. Swimming is good for people who are overweight, who have foot injuries or other orthopedic problems, the arthritic and the handicapped.

Recommendations. Swimming is the best of the aerobics in terms of being the most rhythmical and exercising the most muscle groups, but it expends fewer calories per minute than running. So for overall exercise it beats running, but is not as good for losing weight.

You must have a large enough pool. Most backyard swimming pools are too confining. You could join an adult training program or a community program at your local Y or health club. Belonging to such a program will also give you the proper organization, supervision, and advice you will need to derive the most from your swimming.

Precautions. The common problems that come from swimming are swimmer's ear and eye irritation from chlorine. Of course, if you disregard the usual safety rules around pools, you can injure yourself in other serious ways.

Aerobic Dance

With the popular interest in aerobic exercises of all kinds, aerobic dance was developed to give people a sociable way to exercise. It is a good exercise for people who need group support to maintain interest.

Participants. Anyone who is moderately fit can participate in aerobic dance. It is equally beneficial for all ages.

Recommendations. Dance falls somewhere between walking and running in aerobic capacity if the target heart rate is realized and sustained for thirty consecutive minutes. It can be adapted to overweight people if it is composed of steps that do not lift the body off the floor and lower it too heavily upon the joints. If you are seriously out of shape, you may have to precondition yourself at first just to keep up with your group and not get too winded. For this reason, you should join a class at the appropriate level of your capacity. When you learn the right dance movements, you'll be able to exercise all the muscles of your body, an advantage that dance has over walking and running.

Precautions. Watch out for injuries to the joints of the lower limbs.

Hiking

Hiking is more strenuous than walking and, in the right place, it can be more adventurous. However, some outings that are classified as "hikes," like nature strolls through a local park, only produce aerobic benefits if done strenuously and with more vim than the leisurely walk.

Participants. Anyone who can walk with comfort and ease should be able to go on most hikes. If you have arthritic or other orthopedic disability, you may find that the resistance involved in walking up inclines is too much for you. For this reason, longer, strenuous hikes over hilly terrain should be limited to persons of at least a moderate fitness level.

Recommendations. For short, less vigorous hikes, such as a one-hour nature hike, review the recommendations for walking given above. For full-day hikes or backpacking, plan to prepare yourself physically by walking at a quickened pace for a week or so before you go. You may want to strengthen legs, knees, ankles, and back by doing calisthenics regularly for a week before your hike. Remember that your lower back needs to be strong if you will be carrying a heavy backpack. In general, a rather high level of fitness is needed for long-distance backpacking and all-day hiking.

Precautions. Pay close attention to environmental conditions such as roughness of the terrain, extremes of heat and cold, low tree branches, wild animals. Take adequate water and clothing. Don't forget first aid supplies. Perhaps the most essential piece of equipment for hiking is your boots. Without proper boots hiking can be an excruciating ordeal. The right fit is one that does not squeeze your foot either at the toes or at the heel in climbing up or down hills. Keep in mind that your foot will slide to either end of the boot, depending on whether you are climbing uphill or down. Buy a pair of boots that will minimize this friction that can cause cramping and blisters.

Cross-Country Skiing

Cross-country skiing is a good form of aerobic activity for those who live in the appropriate climate.

Participants. All age groups regardless of skill level. You will get considerable exercise out of skiing whether you are a pro or a beginner. Skiing cross-country does require a moderate level of fitness, however. Skiing does not produce as much trauma to the joints as running does, and it provides exercise for the upper as well as the lower portions of the body.

Recommendations. We suggest you study up on skiing before you try it. Get the proper equipment and adequate instruction. You will also have to familiarize yourself with the trails and hazards of the terrain.

Precautions. Be aware of environmental conditions that in snowy and hilly terrain can sometimes be treacherous. Wear the right clothing to keep warm and dry.

Minitrampoline

You don't have to be an acrobat to profit from trampoline workouts. The more acrobatic you are, however, the more satisfaction you will probably get.

Participants. Persons who engage in minitrampoline exercises need to be well coordinated and have no equilibrium problems. It is an excellent aerobic exercise for individuals who are confined to indoor activity because of the climate or the neighborhood.

Recommendations. Because of its boring nature, many people do not exercise long enough to derive the essential cardiorespiratory benefits from it. Like jumping rope, it takes a certain amount of willpower to persevere at it for the length of time recommended for aerobic training.

Precautions. Trampolines should not be used by children without supervision. The most common problems are injuries to the lower extremities. Sometimes collision with stationary objects like walls and floors is a problem.

*   *   *

From the information given above, you should be able to begin deciding which form of aerobic activity is the right one for you. Whichever you choose, remember that it will not qualify as an aerobic activity that modifies your cardiovascular risk factors if it does not meet the fourfold prescription requirement of mode, duration, frequency, and intensity that we described earlier in this chapter. Of these four, intensity is what really makes or breaks your workout. To exercise at 70 to 85 percent of your maximum heart rate is your target. If you do not meet this target heart rate, your exercising, even though beneficial in other ways, is not true conditioning for your cardiovascular system. Your heart, lungs, and blood vessel system require this strenuous activity to really strengthen themselves to their optimal condition. Exercising at your target heart rate is what produces the training effect that qualifies as aerobic training.

Can I still do push-ups and play softball?

Sure, there are other popular and fun forms of exercise in addition to the aerobic exercises we have been emphasizing in this chapter that can supplement your fitness or weight-reduction program. In themselves, however, they are not the accelerated, steady-state activity that will improve cardiovascular health or reduce your weight. As "companion activities" they are fine and should be encouraged as part of your total exercise program.

Recreational sports. As we have already seen in our graph comparisons, sociable recreational sports, like racketball, volleyball, golf, and bowling, will not raise your target heart rate to a steady level of aerobic activity. They are, though, fun, and force you to move your body, which in itself is important for total fitness. You will also derive a sense of accomplishment in being able to compete with other people physically, and as you become more fit and trim from your aerobic program, these periodic sessions will become easier for you and reinforce your commitment to staying in shape.

Calisthenics, yoga, weight lifting. These types are good for conditioning specific parts of the body—building up muscle tone, firming up saggy areas, and improving your general flexibility. Many people find them boring and reminiscent of unpleasant days in high school gymnasiums or military barracks.

They are hard to stick with. But as part of your total program they should not be disparaged.

Calisthenics make great warm-up exercises. Contrary to what you may have heard, they do not reduce specific spots of the body. Spot reducing is, by and large, a myth. Most calisthenics do not burn fat, rather they tone and strengthen the muscles they work on. Tennis players demonstrate this well. If skin folds are measured on each arm of a tennis player, they will measure the same. In other words, there is the same amount of fat on each arm. But the triceps is larger on the serving arm, as you might imagine.

Yoga (and some calisthenics) will improve your flexibility, allowing for the maximal range of motion through a joint. Yoga is also good for stretching the various muscle groups, releasing tension where it may occur after other forms of exercise, such as in the hamstrings behind your thighs. Devotees of yoga claim better appetite, sounder sleep, peace of mind, and an overall sense of well-being.

Weight lifting can be dangerous without a supervised program. In essence it is the antithesis of aerobic exercise: it requires short bursts of energy; it does not promote steady breathing; it has no effect over the total body unless each and every part of the body is concentrated on with specific exercises to condition that part. Systematic weight lifting will increase the force you can generate from your muscles, thus increasing your strength, and in the process reshaping your body so that it has a more pleasing appearance.

Pleasing, of course, is like beauty. It is in the eye of the beholder. What pleases one does not necessarily please another. Your life should please you, just as the shape of your body when observed in a mirror should please you. I hope your eyes will be opened to the beauty of a vigorous, healthy, active life. You should not settle for less. Your life can be turned into moments of creative, dynamic living. Exercise is something you can literally "put your heart into." In fact, you *must* put your heart into it if you expect your heart to function at its optimal level. You will be pleased at how a healthy heart in a healthy body can be a joy to live with.

An Eight-Week Program for Walking, Running, Biking

Walking

This program is designed for all sedentary people just getting started in renewing fitness. A low-level program is advised for those who have previously been inactive, using a variety of modes—walking, cycling, or swimming.

The program is designed to carry you through eight weeks of progression. If you are not satisfied with your accomplishments at the end of any week, repeat that week until the goals can be easily met. The walking paces are described as "comfortable and brisk." To gauge a brisk walk, compared to slow, the target heart rate is a useful tool.

As we described earlier, the exercise intensity is prescribed between a range of 60 and 85 percent of your predicted maximum heart rate. A minimum 60 percent target heart rate would be a measure of a brisk walk. To calculate your own heart rate, take the predicted maximum heart rate for your age (220 minus age) multiplied by .6. If you reach a higher heart rate, it means you are working at a higher intensity—no need to worry. For the slow-walk interval, simply walk at a comfortable pace.

A walking program can be effective for cardiovascular fitness and maintenance of endurance. Keep in mind that for walking to be effective for cardiovascular fitness you should increase your exercise duration to between forty and sixty minutes and add an extra day during the week.

If more strenuous exercise is desired for greater improvement, you would need to adjust to a more vigorous type of exercise such as swimming, hiking, or jogging.

Week 1:   Walk at a comfortable pace for a total time of 20 minutes.

Week 2:   Walk at a comfortable pace for 5 minutes, then increase speed to a brisk walk for 5 minutes. Alternate walking speeds for 4 sets.

Week 3:   Alternate slow and fast sets of 8 minutes each for 4 sets.

Week 4:   Walk comfortably for 10 minutes, briskly for 10, then repeat.
Week 5:   Walk slowly for 10 minutes, briskly for 15 minutes, slowly for 5.
Week 6:   Walk briskly for 20 minutes continuously.
Week 7:   Walk briskly for 30 minutes continuously.
Week 8:   Walk briskly for 40 minutes continuously.

Running

The running or jogging progression is designed for people wishing to reach a higher level of fitness but who have previously been modestly active. It is the next progression after completing the beginner level.

The purpose is to further improve your cardiovascular fitness. Through this eight-week program the goal is to jog thirty minutes continuously.

Week 1:   Alternate easy jogging and walking for 20 minutes. Begin the aerobic period with walking. Jogging intervals should be no more than 5 minutes at a time during Week 1. When you become winded and tired, slow to a walk. Jog again once you are rested. Repeat Week 1 until you can jog continuously for 5 minutes.
Week 2:   Alternate slow jog and walk for 30 minutes. Begin walking for 5 minutes, then alternate walking with 5 minutes of slow jogging. Total jogging time should be 15 minutes.
Week 3:   Walk briskly for 5 minutes. Jog continuously for 10, walk 5, jog 10. Day 3 of this week add 5 minutes to the jogging interval.
Week 4:   Walk for 5 minutes. Jog at a comfortable pace for 15 minutes, walk for 5 minutes or until rested. Jog 5 minutes, walk 5 for a cool-down.
Week 5:   Walk 5, jog at a comfortable pace for 20 minutes. Slow down toward the end of the period if you need to but try not to break the jog during the 20 minutes. Cool down with a 5-minute walk.
Week 6:   Repeat workout for Week 5.
Week 7:   Walk 5 minutes. The 5-minute walk at the beginning of the session will serve as the warm-up for each day. Also don't forget flexibility exercises prior to the

aerobic phase. Jog slowly for 5 minutes, gradually
increase jogging pace and continue for 25 minutes.
Slow down for another 5 minutes.

Week 8: That is it! After a proper warm-up, jog at a steady,
comfortable pace for 30 minutes. Repeat this workout
until you can run 3 miles in 30 minutes.

Cycling Program

The goal in the cycling program is to condition the thigh
muscles to tolerate increasing amounts of resistance while also
improving cardiovascular fitness. Beginning level for novice
cyclists is not necessary, since there is not the same concern
about joint trauma as there is in starting a running program.

As part of the program, cycle slowly for three minutes before
beginning the workout. At the end of the ride, cycle slowly for
three minutes. You will need to cover more miles on a bike to
gain benefits similar to an aerobic workout on foot, simply
because cycling is at a faster speed. The common factor is
duration, and in this prpgression you will be working up to sixty
minutes. Thirty minutes of continous pedaling at your target
heart rate will be effective for fitness. This is not to be confused
with cycling the required time at a *leisurely* pace. It takes *work*
to pedal at a continuous pace so your heart rate is elevated. The
progression will use *times* as a factor rather than distance.

Week 1: Cycle 20 minutes continuously. Check your pulse
after 10 minutes. Increase pedal speed if you are
under target.

Week 2: Cycle 20 minutes. Check pulse after 10 minutes.
Pedal faster during the second 10-minute segment.
Cool down for 3 minutes.

Week 3: Cycle 30 minutes. Again use the homward-bound
stretch to pump harder and maintain that pace for 15
minutes.

Week 4: Repeat Week 3 but work at a higher intensity during
the full 30-minute session.

Week 5: Lengthen the session by 10 minutes to a total time of
40 minutes. Try to find a moderate incline of uphill
grade during the ride. Pumping uphill is obviously
more demanding and by practicing on hills the benefits for increased fitness are greater.

Week 6: Repeat Week 5.
Week 7: Cycle up to 50 minutes. Remember to monitor your
         pulse and adjust pedal speed accordingly.
Week 8: Cycle continuously for 1 hour.

Fill in the Daily Log on (page 220). The first line has been filled
in as an example.

DAILY LOG

WEEK	DAY	TYPE OF EXERCISE	DISTANCE	TOTAL TIME	CONTINU- OUS TIME	ESTIMATED PACE	EXERCISE HEART RATE
1	1	run	2 miles	22	22	11	25
1	1						
1	2						
1	3						
1	4						
1	5						
1	6						
1	7						
2	1						
2	2						
2	3						
2	4						
2	5						
2	6						
2	7						
3	1						
3	2						
3	3						
3	4						
3	5						
3	6						
3	7						

PART III

Conclusion

11

From Around The Nation

People with heart disease are like travelers on a journey through a desert, a journey with many stops along the way—stops for knowledge, to make a commitment, to express shock, to overcome fear and worry, to find gumption and guts. Pat Taylor is presently stopped at what we might call "an oasis of hope." Others have joined her. But some less fortunate travelers give up at a mirage of despair and defeat. As Pat said, "They think it's too much effort and so they just lie down and die." Of course, there are some people who have no choice. They *are* up against odds that are too great for them, and nothing can be done. They are the patients, truly lost, who never make it.

How we each begin—and end—this journey is unique. Some of us are forced on it cruelly and irrevocably by a heart attack or stroke. Some of us read a book, such as this one, take the Heart Test, and discover we have been on this journey for some time now. The discovery of where each of us is can be a cruel awakening. We know. In the hundreds of cards and letters that came to us after the "20/20" program, we have read the touching, often anguished ways that people from around the nation reacted to their own self-discovery regarding their risk factors for heart disease. We would like to share with you some of these very compelling insights into the struggle with atherosclerosis, our nation's number one killer.

"I scored low; my husband scored high."

What struck us so profoundly about many viewers' reactions was how the family setting is so central in the prevention and treatment of heart disease. Husbands and wives wrote to us about their spouses, their children, their own parents. Whether through heredity or environment, when one member of a family recognizes his or her own potential for heart disease, the entire family must take note. To be orphaned or widowed, to lose a child or a brother or sister—these are most serious events in any family. Even short of death, to live and care for a husband or wife or parent who is a heart victim changes the fabric of life for the entire family. When atherosclerosis disables one family member, no one really "escapes"—because the potential is always there. The risk must be considered, remembered, and dealt with for the rest of one's life.

A disheartening letter came from a woman in West Virginia about her own health and that of her family. She thanked us for the letter that we sent her, confirming her Heart Test score that placed her in a high-risk category. We encouraged her to get medical help, but she wrote back, "I recently found that I have hypoglycemia and am on a strict diet, eating six small meals a day, and must walk three miles every day, but with my husband and mother both having cancer, it is difficult for me to care much about myself." How necessary it is for members of a family to reach out to each other when illness strikes and to care for each other's health as if it were even more important than their own! Despite what at times seem like impossible odds against us, we must continue to believe that there is a way to good health. We are sending the West Virginia woman a copy of this book with the hope that she finds the opportunity to apply this heart-care program to her own life even as she nurses the other members of her family.

"The Heart Test got us both to make some changes."

A Massachusetts man whose wife is a school nurse wrote us that they had made changes in their own ways of living after taking the Heart Test on TV. Their own concern, however, did not stop just with their immediate family. He asked if we would send him more information on the risk factors so that his wife could educate the faculty in her school district. By educating teachers, knowledge and information about heart risks could disseminate down to their students and from them to their parents. Word must go out. We appreciate the efforts of this couple who have joined the cause of reaching as many people as possible to reduce the number of senseless deaths each year from atherosclerosis.

"I have learned so much about heart disease in the last two months."

Not everyone learns easily. A Florida woman wrote that a month after watching the "20/20" program, her husband, a high risk, suffered two heart attacks resulting in open-heart surgery and two coronary arterial bypasses. For her, as well as for her husband, knowledge of heart disease came dramatically and painfully. Her husband is doing fine, but their need to understand heart disease and how to combat it will never be completely over. She ended her letter with the plea, "If there is any additional information which would help my husband to fight this disease, please forward it to us." *Additional information.* In the years to come I'm sure medical science will make additional breakthroughs and we will know a lot more. In the meantime, our goal is to apply all the knowledge we currently have and encourage people to remain steadfast in their commitment to better health. Thousands of people, like this couple, could be living healthier lives free of future heart attacks and strokes—but it takes a commitment, a strong commitment.

"He goes back to work today."

Another woman wrote of her husband's heart attack and surgery after discovering too late on our "20/20" test that he was a high-risk candidate for heart disease. He is now ending a long and troublesome recovery period. Being able to go back to work is a milestone in a patient's fight for health. It signals the resumption of a somewhat normal life again. But in many ways heart victims' lives will never be the same. They will always be shadowed by the threat of another attack and limited by the possibility of an early death. The Heart Test convinced many viewers to begin steps immediately to ward off the evil of that day when risk becomes reality. Numerous letters attested to the importance of "normal" living and of how important it is to safeguard the health necessary for that normal living.

"He died quickly."

Sad, moving letters—and so frustrating from our point of view—came from people who took the Heart Test, realized their high-risk potential, wrote for advice, and suffered their fatal tragedies before we could respond or before they could seek help elsewhere. On the letter we sent to a Colorado man who wrote to us about his own high risk, his wife penned the following brief note and mailed it back to us. "I wanted to inform you that the person you wrote this to died of a heart attack at his home. Though I was here when he got sick, I called for help and gave first aid. He died quickly."

"Just taking it easy now."

This Wisconsin man wrote that our letter came "three weeks too late but thanks just the same." He took the Heart Test on TV in February and wrote us for advice. In March he went to his doctor for a six-month checkup for diabetes. His blood pressure was good and so was his blood sugar level. Two weeks later, even with his "good" reports from his doctor, he had a heart attack. After that, our letter to him arrived. He told us that we had "hit it right on the nose" with our heart questionnaire, while a checkup at his doctor's missed the point altogether. Still, we were too late. He is now waiting for further testing to see how much damage the attack did to his heart. He apologized for the handwritten note because he didn't want to "waste steps to go into the basement and type." Too late he discovered how important each and every step is in the fight against heart disease.

". . . overdosing on aspirin . . ."

A woman in Arkansas had an ECG and sound-wave testing when she became worried about her high score on the Heart Test. She also thought she was having "mild" heart attacks. The intensive screening, however, showed no heart damage. But in the course of her tests, she learned that she had a "mitral valve prolapse," a floppiness or ballooning in the valve that directs the flow of blood between one of the upper and lower chambers of the heart. A malfunctioning mitral valve such as this usually causes no serious problems, but there are precautionary measures that must be taken. With the knowledge of her condition and the necessary follow-up examinations, she will probably lead a normal life. Incidentally, the "mild" heart attacks that led her to seek help in the first place turned out to be stomach pains (acute gastritis) from overdosing on aspirin for her arthritis condition!

"So if there is any way I can lower my risk, please tell me."

This plea came from a Vermont woman who learned for the first time on the "20/20" program how serious the family factor is in heart disease. "My grandparents had heart problems. In fact, my grandfather died of a massive heart attack. My mother also has heart disease." As you know, and as she found out, a family history of heart disease is not a modifiable risk factor. For people like this New England woman, a consistent and systematic effort to reduce their *other* risk factors is their best hope. And we all must begin early, not just in the prevention of heart disease but in every aspect of our lives that touches upon our health in any way. We do not want to end up like another woman, in rural Pennsylvania, who wrote that she had been "bad sick for a long time" with nausea, vomiting, diarrhea, shortness of breath, no appetite, and a weight loss of twenty-seven pounds in three weeks. When she wrote us with her test score, we responded with a letter that she was indeed at high risk and should get medical attention. We hope that she not only overcomes her illness but makes the necessary changes in her life so that these symptoms do not recur.

One young man with four children reported to us a high Heart Test score of 55. We suggested a cardiovascular screening immediately not only for him but, even more importantly, for his children, who already have an increased risk from the hereditary standpoint. We were not shocked to find high cholesterol, high triglycerides, and low HDLs in each child. Their challenge for the future is clear: Accept the fact that they come from a family with heart disease but do not accept it as inevitable for themselves. Under the proper program, they can reduce and eventually eliminate the risk factors that are under their control.

"I plan to be around a lot longer!"

On a positive note, a forty-four-year-old married woman in Virginia, the mother of two teenage children, responded that she knew when she took the Heart Test that she was a heart patient. She had diabetes and high blood pressure, among other risk factors, but she thought her heart condition "would never be noticed." The Heart Test convinced her otherwise. Today she is under the care of a good doctor and, because her condition was detected in time and treated competently, she can write, "I plan to be around a lot longer!"

It is as simple as that—and as difficult as that. You must plan to be around a lot longer, and then put that plan into practice. Make it a plan of action, not just a vague wish or desire for a longer and healthier life. Take your results from the Heart Test and make them produce *results in your life.* Take seriously the risk factors that threaten your life. Don't wander aimlessly as if lost and looking for a way out of the wilderness, as if there are no guideposts, no directions, no compass. There are. A heart-care program such as the one outlined in this book can reduce your risk factors and put you on the road to better health.

Learn all you can about the prevention of heart disease, learn what *you* personally must *do* to prevent atherosclerosis from diminishing the quality of your life and that of your family. Then *do it,* and live so that you too will be around a lot longer.

Index

ABC Television Network, 3,
    21, 47
Absolutistic thinking, 95–96
Accelerated atherosclerosis, 30
Accountability, 108
Addiction, psychological, to
    smoking, 62
Adrenaline
    anger and, 97
    irrational thinking and, 93
Aerobic dance, 211–12
Aerobic exercise, 22, 188,
    193–94
    action on heart of, 195–96, 197
    blood pressure lowered by,
        198
    choice of, 207–8
    for heart patients, 196–97
    intensity of target heart rate
        in, 201
    modes of, 199
    resting heart rate lowered by, 200

for weight reduction, 146, 147,
    195
Age, risk factors associated with,
    28–30, 36
Airplanes, meals on, 166
Albrecht, Karl, 108
Alcohol, 164
    benefits of moderate intake
        of, 157
Alternate nostril breathing
    exercise, 91
American Diabetic Association
    Food Exchange Lists,
    126–30
Anaerobic exercise, 194–95
Anger, 97–100
Angina, 6, 10, 11
    history of, 32, 33
    triggered by stress, 17
Angry thinking, 86
Antacids, low-sodium, 178

Arizona Heart Institute, 3, 5, 10, 11, 13, 14, 17–18, 43, 53, 111
  diets of, 155, 156, 165, 176
  exercise programs of, 208
  fitness profiles at, 191
  quit-smoking program of, 67–73
  research at, 158
  weight management program of, 112, 146
Artificial sweeteners, 161
Assertiveness techniques, 121–22
Atherosclerosis, 6, 11, 51, 224, 225, 228
  accelerated, 30
  aging and, 29–30
  alcohol and, 157
  angina and, 33
  childhood, 31–32
  diet and, 152, 153, 155, 158
  Diethrich Program for, 11–14
  genetic factors in, 30–31
  Heart Test scores for patients with, 21
  major risk factors for, 19
  prevention of progression of, 16
Atkins diet, 155, 157

Backpacking, 212
"Banking" calories, 119
Barnard, Christian, 75
"Baseline Stimuli Record" (AHI quit-smoking program), 68, 69
Basic food groups, 125, 152, 153
Baylor College of Medicine, 29
Beef, limiting intake of, 162
Behavioral stress cues, 82
Behavior modification, 11, 13
  in quitting smoking, 67
  for Type A's, 101–3

for weight reduction, 112, 116–24
Beverages, 186
Beverly Hills diet, 155
Biking, 209–10
  eight-week program of, 218–19
Binge eating, elimination of, 117
Biofeedback training, 22
Blood analysis, 13, 15
Blood fat levels, 20, 44
  elevated, diet for people with, 158–71
Blood pressure
  control of, 14
  high, see High blood pressure
  in response to exercise, 15
  weight reduction and, 113
Blood sugar, lowering of, 157
Breads, 183
  for weight-reduction, diet, 129
Breath-counting exercise, 90
Breathing exercises, relaxation through, 90–91
Bruce Protocol, 15
Bypass surgery, 7, 9, 10, 11
  recurrence of, 12

Caffeine, 164
Calendars, learning to use, 105–6
Calesthenics, 194, 199, 214–15
Calories
  "banking," 119
  definition of, 124–25
  excess, 153
  exercise equivalents of, 148–49
  in fat, 154
  See also Low-calorie diet
Carbohydrates, 44, 154
  refined, 161–65
  unrefined, 164
Carbon monoxide, 56
Cardiologists, 13
Cardiopulmonary resuscitation (CPR), 22

Catastrophizing, 86
Catheterization, 13, 16
Character diagnosis, 96–97
Cheese, 162, 179–80
Chest pain
  causes of, 32–33
  See also Angina
Childhood atherosclerosis,
    31–32
Chocolate, 164
Cholesterol levels, 10, 13, 15,
    19, 44
  diet and, 152
  influence of exercise on, 198
  family environment and, 31–32
  reduction of, 126–31, 154,
    157, 158–65
  as risk factor, 38
  saturated fats and, 160, 161–65
  smoking and, 56, 74
  of Type A's, 101
  weight reduction and, 113
Cilia, 57
Cognitive psychotherapy, 93
Collateral circulation, 33
  exercises to increase, 197
Compliments, learning to accept,
    122
Condiments, 186
  for low-sodium diets, 174,
    175, 176
Confusion, stress related to,
    86
Congenital heart problems, 33
Conscious eating, 117
Cooley, Denton, 207
Cooper, Kenneth, 188
Craving for cigarettes, 62
Cross-country skiing, 213
"Crutch," smoking as, 61–62
Cycling, *see* Biking

Daily exercise log, 220
Dance, aerobic, 211–12
DeBakey, Michael, 29
Delegation of tasks, 106
Desserts, 164, 185

Diabetes, 6, 20
  eating habits and, 32
  obesity and, 153
  as risk factor, 37
Dichotomous thinking, 86
Diet, 11, 20, 151–86
  acceptable snacks for, 165
  chart of foods allowed and
    not allowed on, 178–86
  cholesterol in, 159
  eating out and, 166–69
  for entire family, 12, 17
  fats in, 160
  low-fat, low-sodium,
    low-refined carbohydrate,
    13–14, 158–71
  low-sodium, 171–78
  modification of, 22
  refined carbohydrates in, 161
  as risk factor, 38–39
  for weight reduction, 113,
    124–45
Diet-Weight History Inventory,
    113–15
Diethrich Diet, 156, 157, 158
Diethrich Program, 11–14
Diet soda, 186
  sodium in, 174
Downs, Hugh, 3

Eating out, *see* Restaurants
Education
  on nutrition, 155
  in weight reduction program,
    113
Eggs, 162, 179
Electrocardiograms (ECG), 13, 15
Ellis, Albert, 93–94
Emotional-cognitive stress cues,
    80
Emotions
  heart as seat of, 25
  stress and, 92–94
Endurance, 190
Environment
  family, 31–32
  for weight reduction, 118–19

Epictetus, 92, 93

Estrogen, 28

Evening snacks, 119

Exercise, 11, 13, 20, 22,
   187–219
  aerobic dance, 211–12
  biking, 209–10, 218–19
  for blood pressure control, 14
  breathing, for relaxation,
    90–91
  consulting with doctor on,
    189–90
  cross-country skiing, 213
  daily log for, 220
  duration of, 199, 204
  eight-week programs of,
    216–17
  exhaustion and, 197
  family patterns of, 31–32
  frequency of, 199–200, 204
  general guidelines for, 206–7
  HDL level and, 157–58
  for heart patients, 196–97
  high levels of, 16
  hiking, 212–13
  illness and, 197–98
  intensity of, 200–4
  lap swimming, 211
  minitrampoline, 213–14
  modes of, 199
  outlook on life improved by,
    187–88
  peak heart rate during, 15
  and quitting smoking, 73
  risk factor of lack of, 40,
    44, 46
  running, 188, 217–18
  taking time for, 107
  walking, 208–9, 216–17
  warming up for, 204–5
  for weight reduction, 113,
    145–49

Fad diets, 154–55

Family history of heart disease,
   30–32, 36, 44

Fats, 130, 159–60, 184–85

  calorie concentration in, 154
  foods high in, 153

Faulty thinking
  absolutistic and moralistic,
    95–96
  character diagnosis in, 96–97
  global, nondimensional, 94–95
  inventory of, 85–87
  in irreversible frame, 96
  techniques to overcome,
    91–97

Finland, coronary disease in,
   22

Fish, 181–82

Fitness profiles, 191

Fix-it manuals, 45

Flexibility, 191

Flex time, 107

Fluids
  diets restricting, 155
  retention of, 28, 152–53, 172

Food exchange lists, 126–30

Food shopping, 117–18

Four basic food groups, 125,
   152, 153

Franklin, Ben, 71

Free foods, 131

Free time, 107

Friedman, Meyer, 100–2

Frost, Robert, 95

Fruit, 127–28, 164, 184

Frustration, stress as response
   to, 76–77

Gender, risk factors of, 27–28, 36

Global framework, 94

Grocery store temptations, 117–18

Habit, smoking from, 62

HDLs, 13, 15, 30, 157–58
  influence of exercise on, 198

Heart attacks, 19
  anger of victims of, 97–98
  decline in number of deaths
    from, 22
  diet and, 157–58
  fear of recurrence of, 187–88

Heart attacks *(cont.)*
  gender and, 27–28
  genetic tendency in, 30
  history of, 20, 32–33
  returning to work after, 109
  technology and, 192–93
  Type A behavior and, 100–1
Heart-lung machine, 26
Heart Test, 3, 6, 10, 15, 16, 19, 35–41, 45–47
  accuracy of, 21
  anger at results of, 97–98
  blood pressure rating on, 171–72
  diet and, 151, 158
  exercise score on, 187–89
  high scores on, consultation with doctor indicated by, 43
  philosophy of, 26–27
  responses to, 223–28
  weight score on, 111, 113
Heart transplants, 10, 29, 75
High blood pressure, 20
  aging and, 29
  diet for people with, 171–81
  family environment and, 31–32
  obesity and, 46
  oral contraceptives and, 28
  as risk factor, 39
  smoking and, 74
  sodium and, 152
  among Type A's, 101
High density lipoproteins, *see* HDLs
Hiking, 212–13
Holistic approach, 23, 47
Human contact at work, 109
Hypertension, *see* High blood pressure
Hypochondriacal thinking, 87

Ideal weight, 14, 15
  attainment of, *see* Weight reduction
  maintenance of, 153–54

Illness
  exercise and, 197–98
  taking time to recuperate from, 107
Inderal, 10
International Heart Foundation, 158
Interpretation of events, 92–95
Irrational ideas, stress-producing, 93–94
Irreversible frame of thinking, 96
Ischemia, 197
Isometrics, 199

James I, King of England, 54
Job status, 108

Kennedy, John F., 17
Konishi, Frank, 149

Labels, how to read, 125, 169–71
Lap swimming, 211
Lipoproteins, *see* HDLs
Low-calorie diet, 124–45
  exercise and, 146, 147
  food exchange lists, 126–30
  1,000-calorie plan, 132–35
  1,200-calorie plan, 135–38
  1,400-calorie plan, 138–42
  snacks and, 141–42, 144–45
Low self-confidence, 85–86
Lungs, effect of smoking on, 57

Margarine, 163
Marvell, Andrew, 101
Meals
  scheduling of, 117
  social element of, 156
  taking time for, 107
Meats, 130, 162
  cooking methods for, 163
  high in cholesterol, 180–81
  lower in cholesterol, 181–82
  unrefined carbohydrates as replacement for, 164
Medical history, 32–33, 37, 44

Medical monitoring, 13
Medication, 7, 10
  for blood pressure control, 14
  elimination of need for, 14,
    16
Meditation seminars, 22
Memories, eating style influenced
    by, 115–16
Menopause, 28
Mental challenge of work, 109
Methodist Hospital (Houston), 29
Mexican restaurants, 167
Midnight snacks, 119–20
Milk, 126, 178–79
  skimmed, 162
Milton, John, 47
Moralistic thinking, 95–96
Moving slowly, relaxation
    through, 89
Mu, 102

National Academy of Sciences,
    171
Negative feelings, smoking to
    reduce, 61–62, 63
Negativistic thinking, 86
Nervousness after quitting
    smoking, 73
Nicotine, 55
  blood vessels constricted by,
    56
Nondimensional frame of
    thought, 94–95
Noninvasive screening
    procedures, 10
Nuclear scanning, 13, 15
Nutrition, 13, 154–55
Nutritionists, 13
Nuts, 163

Obesity, 10, 20
  diseases associated with, 153
  family patterns of, 31–32
  health problems correlated
    with, 112
  as risk factor, 39–40, 44, 46
Open-heart surgery, 9, 10, 21

Oral contraceptives, 28
Organ meats, 162
Oriental restaurants, 166–67
Oxygen, 56

Pasta, 182–83
Phrases, relaxation, 89–90
Physical challenge of work, 109
Physical fitness, 188–89
  average level of, 192
  components of, 190–91
  negative influence of
    technology on, 192–93
  satisfaction with level of, 191
Physical stress cues, 80–81
  relaxation techniques to
    combat, 88–91
Physical work environment, 108
Physiologists, 13, 16
Pleasure, smoking as accentuation
    of, 61
Polyphasic thinking, 85
Polyunsaturated fats, 160, 163
Potatoes, 182–83
Poultry, 180–82
Preventive medicine, 20, 23
  latest developments in, 43
  risk factors and, 45
Pritikin diet, 14
Pritikin, Nathan, 157, 158
Psychological addiction to
    smoking, 62
Psychologists, 13

Quality of life, 17, 18, 23
  diet and, 156, 158

Recreational sports, 199, 214
Red blood cells, 56
Reduction of negative feelings,
    smoking for, 61–62, 63
Refined carbohydrates, 161
  diet low in, 161–65
Registered nurses, 13
Relaxation
  inventory on, 83–85
  smoking for, 61

Relaxation *(cont.)*
taking time for, 107
techniques for, 88–90
Responsibility, excessive, 86
Restaurants, staying on diet
when eating in, 120–21,
166–69
Resting ECGs, 13, 15
Rice, 182–83
Risk factors, 20
of age, 28–30
in family, 30–32
of gender, 27–28
Heart Test assessment of,
36–41
in medical history, 32–33
nonmodifiable, 27–33
reduction of, 13, 43–48,
51
Roosevelt, Teddy, 193
Rope jumping, 210
Rosenman, Ray, 100
Running, 208
eight-week program of,
217–18

Salad dressing, 163
Salt substitutes, 174
Sample meal plans
1,000-calorie, 133–35
1,200-calorie, 135–38
1,400-calorie, 138–41
Santayana, George, 32
Saturated fats, 126, 160, 163,
164, 184
Scarsdale diet, 155, 157
Self-confidence, 85–86
Self-reference, 86
Self-support, 122–24
Selye, Hans, 77
Shellfish, 162
Shopping for food, 117–18
Shrimp, 162
Side-stream smoking, 54, 55
Skiing, cross-country, 213
Skin fold measurement, 14
Skippies, 16

Smoking, 6, 14, 20, 45, 53–74
esthetic disadvantages of, 66
exercise and, 207
from habit, 62
handling cigarette as reason
for, 61
health damage from, 56–57,
66
mastery of dependence on,
67
for pleasurable relaxation, 61
programs for quitting, 67–72
psychological addiction to,
62
quiz on changing habits of,
63–65
reasons given for, 55–56
for reduction of negative
feelings, 61–62
as risk factor, 37–38
score analysis on, 60
setting good example by giving
up, 66
side effects of quitting, 73
for stimulation, 60–61
test on feelings about, 57–59
by Type A's, 101
by women, 28
Snacks, 119–20
acceptable, 165
common, calorie values of,
142–44
low-calorie, 141–42, 144–45
salt content of, 173–74
Sodium
diet low in, 171–78
high blood pressure and, 152
limit on intake of, 154
Softened water, 174
Soul, association of heart with,
25–26
Soups, 163, 185
salt content of, 174
Stillman diet, 155
Stimulation, smoking for,
60–61
Stimuli to eating, 117

Stoics, 93
Strength, 190
Strenuous exercise, 193
Stress, 20, 75–109
   anger and, 97–100
   angina triggered by, 17
   behavioral cues of, 82
   emotional-cognitive cues of,
      80
   exercise to alleviate, 198
   family patterns of, 31–32
   faulty thinking as cause of,
      85–87
   frustration and helplessness
      as source of, 76–77
   indicators of, 78–79
   inventories on, 80–88
   physical cues of, 80–81
   reduction of, 13, 14, 22
   relaxation and, 83–85, 88–90
   response of heart to, 79–80
   as risk factor, 41
   time use and, 87–88, 103–6
   Type A behavior and,
      82–83, 100–3
   women under, 28
   at work, 108–9
Stress ECGs, 13, 15
Strokes, 19
   decline in number of deaths
      from, 22
   diet and, 158
   gender and, 27–28
   genetic tendency in, 30
   history of, 32–33
   Type A behavior and, 101
Sugar levels, 15
   weight reduction and, 113
Support system for weight
      reduction, 121–24
Surgery, program to
      complement results of, 11–12
Sweets, 185–86
   avoidance of, 161–62
Swimming, 211

Target heart rate, 200–2

Tasks
   delegation of, 106
   variety of, 108–9
Taylor, Pat, 5–12, 14–18, 223
Team sports, 194
Technology, fitness reduced
      by, 192–93
Teenagers, smoking by, 53
Thinking, stress-related, *see*
      Faulty thinking
Time use, 87–88, 103–6
   calendars as planning aid in,
      105–6
   delegation of tasks and, 106
   exercise and, 198
Touching your breathing
      (exercise), 90–91
Transition time between tasks,
      107
Treadmill tests, 13, 15
Triglyceride levels, 13, 15
   build up of, 19
   diet and, 152
   family eating habits and,
      32
   reduction of, 157
   weight reduction and, 113
Twain, Mark, 103
''20/20'' (TV program), 3, 20,
      21, 47, 223–27
Type A behavior, 6, 16, 100–3
   in family environment, 31
   inventory of, 82–83
   techniques for modification of,
      102–3

Unrefined carbohydrates, 164
Urge-Reduction Statement Card
      (AHI quit-smoking
      program), 69
U.S. Senate Select Committee
      on Nutrition and Human
      Needs, 153

Vasodilator, alcohol as, 157
Vegetables, 126–27, 164, 183–84
   for low-sodium diet, 174

Walking, 208–9
  eight-week program of, 216–17
Weight gain after quitting
    smoking, 73
Weight, ideal, *see* Ideal weight
Weight lifting, 214
Weight reduction, 111–49
  aerobic exercise for, 195
  change in eating style for,
    116–17
  dangers of unsupervised, 112
  diet for, 124–45
  Diet-Weight History
    Inventory for, 113–15
  environment for, 118–19
  through exercise, 145–49
  food shopping for, 117–18
  HDL level and, 157–58

  and memories influencing
    eating style, 115–16
  restaurant meals and, 120–21
  snacking and, 119–20
  support system for, 121–24
Westin, Av, 47
Whitman, Walt, 102
Women
  increase in heart disease
    among, 27–28
  smoking by, 53
Work stress, 108–9
World War II, 152

Yoga, 22, 91
  for exercise, 214, 215

Zen, 22, 102

ABOUT THE AUTHOR

Dr. Edward B. Diethrich is the Medical Director of the world-famous Arizona Heart Institute, a diagnostic and treatment center for heart disease. An internationally distinguished surgeon, he has presented hundreds of programs throughout the United States and abroad. He lectures widely and makes frequent appearances on national television. Dr. Diethrich lives in Scottsdale, Arizona.

An Overview

The Wyoming Valley is the home of one of the most ambitious heart health programs ever initiated in the United States.

One out of every two American deaths each year is from heart disease. In our area, the numbers are higher. We are concerned and scared at such a prospect. Something must be done. Between June 19 and August 15 we will address, head on, this devastating common threat. Unlike most preventive health care programs, we are focusing on the community as a whole rather than on single isolated incidences. Under the direction of Edward B. Diethrich and the internationally renowned Arizona Heart Institute (AHI), the Wyoming Valley will embark on an unparalleled eight-week heart health awareness and fitness program. From the sidelines, the nation will watch and wait as we prepare to stalk this silent, powerful killer.

Beginning with the distribution of a simple 12 question test, tens of thousands of area residents will have the opportunity to evaluate and understand their heart health. Our self-assessment survey will allow each participant to determine whether he is a LOW, MEDIUM or HIGH risk. All tests will be collected and the results will be forwarded to AHI for further analysis. All confirmed high risk participants will receive a letter advising that they see their physicians as soon as possible. We believe this aspect alone may well save the lives of hundreds of our neighbors who were unaware of their potential risk.

"Intervention" distinguishes our Project from other community wide studies. Our focus is concise and our response is private sector. Consolidation of community resources is the key. By uniting our skills, talents, and assets we will alert all Valley residents of the five modifiable risk factors: 1.) stress, 2.) smoking, 3.) weight, 4.) diet/nutrition, and 5.) exercise/fitness. The conclusion of our campaign will be a second testing, intended to measure the impact of our heart health awareness program. Our aim is significant short-term improvement but with long-term residual effect on the life styles and general health of our area residents.

A PBS television special, scheduled to air in 1986, will bring our local efforts to national attention. Presenting an image of confidence and pride to a prime time audience is a motivating force behind our Project. The film will record our precedent-setting response for the rest of the country. Communities will look, learn, and listen to the Wyoming Valley's lead.

Such is the ambitious and worthwhile opportunity which lies so firmly within our grasp.

OK, Wyoming Valley, HERE'S OUR CHANCE!

WHY THE WYOMING VALLEY?

"The Valley with a Heart" is more than a slogan or a title we bestowed upon ourselves in a moment of glory.

"The Valley with a Heart" describes a people who have united in a time of crisis. A people who have combined their individual resources for the sake of the community. A people who are concerned about the well-being of others. A people who have "heart."

The most suitable place for a community-wide campaign to combat heart disease is the Wyoming Valley. Where else would people be so willing to join together for a common cause? The scars of Agnes are both painful and comforting: out of the tremendous suffering and anguish we withstood, a certain joy and strength can be found in the memory of the support of our neighbors. With this behind us, we have always been willing to assist in the needs of our community. Together, we have the power to reduce the risks of heart disease. Together, we can fight back!

The OK-Heart Project is not government-funded. Our Board of Directors is composed of a cross-section of Wyoming Valley leaders who are concerned about the alarming statistics of heart disease in our area. We know the strength of our community's dedication to its citizens, and the OK-Heart Project gives us the opportunity to reinforce this belief—to ourselves and our nation.

Once again, the community is calling upon its citizens to unite. This effort to fight heart disease could have happened someplace else. But it didn't. It's happening in the Wyoming Valley. The place where people work together. The place where people are concerned. The Valley with a Heart.

OKheart, Inc.

STAFF

George Culver, Executive Director
Ann Mermelstein, Associate Director
Beth Giebus, Communications Coordinator
Elizabeth Gricol, Marketing Coordinator
Kimberly Radnor, Promotions Coordinator
Mark Thomas, Public Relations Coordinator
Genevieve Mrackoski, Administrative Assistant

LOANED EXECUTIVES

Deborah Hufford, Bell of Pennsylvania
Jane Machinchak, General Hospital
Leona Novak, Wilkes-Barre City Hall
John Nowicki, Mercy Hospital
Diane Shinal, Nesbitt Memorial Hospital

We are grateful to numerous individuals and organizations without whose support, the OK-Heart Project would not have been possible.